Torture

Human rights, medical ethics
and the case of Israel

This book is dedicated to those who have suffered torture at the hands of Israeli interrogators

To the question why I had given false confessions, I told him that I had given these as a result of torture and confinement. When I was questioned as to why I had given the names of my friends, I told them that only my friends could understand my situation and forgive me.

Ismail El-Gul

Torture

Human rights, medical ethics and the case of Israel

Edited by
NEVE GORDON &
RUCHAMA MARTON

With the assistance of
Jon Jay Neufeld

 Zed Books
LONDON AND NEW JERSEY

in association with

the Association of Israeli-Palestinian
Physicians for Human Rights
TEL AVIV

Torture: human rights, medical ethics and the case of Israel
was first published by Zed Books Ltd,
165 First Avenue, Atlantic Highlands,
New Jersey 07716, USA, in 1995.

Copyright © Individual contributors, 1995.
Editorial copyright © Neve Gordon and Ruchama Marton, 1995.

Cover designed by Andrew Corbett.
Set in Monotype Ehrhardt by Ewan Smith, London E8.
Printed and bound in the United Kingdom
by Biddles Ltd, Guildford and King's Lynn.

A catalogue record for this book is
available from the British Library.

US CIP data is available from the Library of Congress.

ISBN 1 85649 313 X Cased
ISBN 1 85649 314 8 Limp

Contents

Foreword

This book is part of an ongoing campaign against the systematic practice of torture by Israeli security forces in Israel and the Occupied Territories. It follows up on the Conference on the International Struggle against Torture and the Case of Israel, held in Tel Aviv on 13–14 June 1993, organized by the Association of Israeli-Palestinian Physicians for Human Rights and the Public Committee against Torture in Israel. Assembling over 450 participants from Israel, the Occupied Territories and abroad, the conference consisted of lectures delivered by local and international experts, workshops designed to produce strategies for the continued struggle against torture, testimonies of torture, a panel discussion between members of the Israeli parliament and Palestinian leaders, and comments from the floor.

Rather than a word-for-word transcription of the proceedings, the book is a presentation of the major issues dealt with at the conference. The contents of the book have been organized in four parts, each one dealing with a major aspect of the practice of torture, discussed by leading figures in the medical, legal and academic fields. Each part consists of chapters providing a theoretical analysis of the issue, concluded by action-oriented recommendations taken from the conference's working groups. This combination and balance of an academic approach with practical prescriptions for action make the book unique.

The main text is followed by three appendices. These provide a general overview of international codes pertaining to torture, and evidence of the practice of torture in Israel and the struggle against it. It is intended that readers will be able to use the appendices as efficient tools in the battle against torture.

We hope that this book will help generate a public outcry against the practice of torture in Israel and around the world.

The Editors

Acknowledgements

We owe a major debt to the many individuals who helped make the Conference on the International Struggle against Torture and the Case of Israel a reality. Without them, this book would not exist. Members of the staff of the Association of Israeli-Palestinian Physicians for Human Rights were indispensable in the organization of the conference; Sharon Shalev did an exceptional job in managing the bulk of the organizational details; and significant contributions were also made by Nogah Ofer and Saleh Haj Yechye. Hanna Friedman and Miriam Frank, from the Public Committee against Torture in Israel, also lent considerable assistance.

Concerning the book itself, Catherine Rottenberg deserves our gratitude for the work she contributed to the appendices.

The conference and the publication of this book were made possible by the support of many individual donors and the following organizations: Agir Ensemble pour les Droits de l'Homme, France; Commission on Interchurch Aid of the Netherlands Reformed Church; Embassy of Switzerland in Israel; International Committee of the Red Cross, Switzerland; Internationale Liga Für Menschenrechte, Germany; International Rehabilitation Council for Torture Victims, Denmark; Medical Foundation for the Care of Victims of Torture, UK; Mission and World Service, Reformed Churches of Netherlands; Physicians for Human Rights, USA.

Abbreviations

AAAS	American Association for the Advancement of Science
BMA	British Medical Association
CIOMS	Council for International Organizations on Medical Sciences
ECPT	European Committee for the Prevention of Torture
GSS	General Security Services (Israel)
ICRC	International Committee of the Red Cross
IDF	Israeli Defence Force
IMA	Israeli Medical Association
MASA	Medical Association of South Africa
PHR	Association of Israeli-Palestinian Physicians for Human Rights
RCT	Rehabilitation and Research Center for Torture Victims (Denmark)
TMA	Turkish Medical Association
WMA	World Medical Association

Contributors

Dr Mamduch Al-Aker is a practising urologist and was head of the human rights committee in the Palestinian delegation to Washington, DC. He is an active member of the Association of Israeli-Palestinian Physicians for Human Rights.

Helen Bamber is the founder and director of the Medical Foundation for the Care of Victims of Torture, UK. She was formerly secretary of the Medical Campaign of the British Medical Group of Amnesty International and the co-founder of the National Association for the Welfare of Hospitalized Children.

Dr Soren Bojholm is chief of psychiatry at the Rehabilitation and Research Center for Torture Victims (RCT/IRCT), Denmark. He has researched in the field of psychiatric rating scales and epidemiology. He is a member of the Danish Psychiatric Association.

Dr Stanley Cohen is a professor of criminology at Hebrew University – School of Law, Israel. He is co-founder of the Public Committee against Torture in Israel. Dr Cohen has also published several books and co-authored the B'Tselem reports on the torture and ill-treatment of Palestinian detainees.

Avigdor Feldman is a practising attorney in Israel and in the past was the head attorney for the Association of Civil Rights in Israel. He is a recipient of the Kennedy Prize for Human Rights.

Dr Jonathan E. Fine, founder and former director of Physicians for Human Rights, USA, is at present senior medical consultant for the organization as well as founder and director of International Witness.

Dr Inge Genefke is medical director of the Rehabilitation and Research Center for Torture Victims, Denmark. She has received numerous international awards in recognition of her work for the rehabilitation of torture victims.

Dr Haim Gordon is a professor of philosophy at Ben Gurion University, Israel, and was founder of the Gaza Team for Human Rights. He has written numerous books, the last two of which deal with political evil in Israel.

Neve Gordon is director of the Association of Israeli-Palestinian Physicians for Human Rights. He is a regular contributor to *Challenge* magazine.

Dr Robert Kirschner is a forensic pathologist and deputy chief medical examiner of Cook County, Chicago, USA. He is also on the faculty of the pathology department at the University of Illinois and a member of the executive committee of Physicians for Human Rights, USA.

Felicia Langer was a practising attorney in Israel for twenty-five years. In the past two years she has been lecturing at Bremen University, Germany. She was the 1990 laureate of the Right Livelihood Award (known as the Alternative Nobel Prize) and has written several books.

Dr Ruchama Marton is a practising psychiatrist. She is founder and chairwoman of the Association of Israeli-Palestinian Physicians for Human Rights. Dr Marton has written numerous papers related to medicine and human rights.

Dahlia Rabikovitch is one of Israel's leading poets. She has published six books of poetry and is represented in numerous anthologies.

Dr Hernan Reyes is medical coordinator for detention-related activities for the International Committee of the Red Cross, Geneva, Switzerland. He has written articles for professional journals.

Dr Eyad El Sarraj is a practising psychiatrist. He is founder and director of the Gaza Community Mental Health Programme and has extensively researched the question of mental health in the Gaza Strip.

Lea Tsemel is a practising attorney in Israel, specializing in cases concerning the violation of Palestinian human rights. She is co-founder of the Public Committee against Torture in Israel.

James Welsh is medical office coordinator at Amnesty International, London, UK, and was the working party consultant behind the book *Medicine Betrayed* (London, Zed Books, 1992).

1 Introduction

RUCHAMA MARTON

In the beginning of 1988, as a reaction to the ever growing rumours of atrocities and brutal acts perpetrated by Israeli soldiers against Palestinians, I organized a group of twelve fellow physicians, and together we drove down to Gaza to see what was actually going on there.

We visited Shifa governmental hospital, where we saw people with multiple fractures of the arms and legs. We saw a 13-year-old boy whose hand was broken in three places. I asked him what had happened to him, and he raised the hand with the cast in a defensive motion. His father told me that the boy's hand had been broken when he tried to defend himself against blows directed to his head. We saw people who had been riddled with bullets that exploded inside their bodies and caused injuries to kidneys, liver and intestines. We saw people in prolonged comas after being beaten on their heads.

Shifa Hospital reeked from overflowing toilets, accumulated filth, bandages stained with blood and pus, and damp and mouldy walls. Israeli hospitals are so different from what we encountered at Shifa that it was hard for us to imagine that this stinking, damp and overcrowded place was indeed a hospital.

We heard stories, and we saw more than we could take in. After the visit, we sat at a gas station on the Israeli side of the border and discussed our reactions to the visit. There, at the gas station at kibbutz Yad Mordechai, we came to the joint conclusion that we could no longer keep silent in the face of such brutality. That was the inception of the group that later came to be known as the Association of Israeli-Palestinian Physicians for Human Rights.

At the beginning of 1992, I was called upon to examine a Palestinian prisoner released on probation. I met a young man who looked like a boy sitting in a wheelchair. His left hand was held close to his chest in a strange position, motionless. His left leg, too, was motionless. On his chest were marks of burns in the shape of parallel stripes caused by an electric heater pressed against his body, and on his hands were circular burns. His face looked serene, and he smiled all the time. Lamia Jaber, then aged 25, had been brutally tortured for months in an Israeli prison. As a result he suffered from hysterical paralysis in his hand and leg.

Seeing Lamia gave me a tremendous shock. This was my first encounter with someone who had undergone torture. My shock and horror intensified upon hearing the reactions of people with whom I discussed Lamia Jaber's torture: 'This is an exceptional case; there's no torture in Israel.'

'An exception to the rule' is an expression commonly used to lull public opinion. Even when the public is informed of a blatant human rights violation, such as the breaking of arms and legs, the poisoning of wheat fields or the death of a detainee under interrogation, the official line is always: This is not the accepted norm of behaviour; this is an exception; our collective political, military and personal behaviour is unobjectionable.

In Israel, the term 'Occupation' is used in a similar way to the phrase 'exception to the rule', except that its target audience is different. 'Exception to the rule' is the sop used by the nationalist camp and the larger segment of the population that constitutes the 'middle ground' – those who are not politically aware. The term 'Occupation', however, is a sop used by the left-wing Zionist camp. The evils that we witness and create are supposedly the result of the Occupation. The Occupation is presented as a kind of a mystical law, an inevitability; everything is the fault of the Occupation. If only the Occupation were done away with, all other evils, brutality, folly and malice would disappear. This line of thinking is prevalent in, and strongly adhered to by, the respectable liberal segment of Israeli society. It prevents one from seeing the wider, deeper context of our life here in Israel. The 'exception to the rule' and the 'Occupation', each in its way and with its specific audience, enable many well-meaning Israelis to exempt themselves from the responsibility of maintaining human rights.

However, the most discouraging reaction was that of total disbelief: I was lying; Lamia was faking. I even heard the claim that Lamia had caused his own burns. Still, the most common reaction was outright denial: there is no torture in Israel. A glaring example of this attitude is the comment of the Israeli Defence Force (IDF) commander of the northern sector who appeared on a television talk show with me and with a catatonic Palestinian, a torture victim. We were all sitting in the same room, the television cameras focusing on the tortured person, his blank eyes staring into space. And the commander pronounced: 'I cannot accept the claim that there is torture in the State of Israel.' The studio audience clapped.

Coming face to face with Lamia's pain, suffering, mental distress, loneliness and helplessness, on the one hand, and with Israeli society's denial, self-deception and cover-up of atrocities, on the other, I experienced the same feelings of pain and disillusionment that I had gone through many years earlier.

Like most of my contemporaries, I was brought up to believe several myths: equality, 'purity of weapons', moral Jewish superiority; the myth that we risk total annihilation and the myth of an empty desert that the Zionists redeemed and turned into a blooming garden. I believed these myths with all my mind and heart. I internalized them and made them part of my personality and the basis of my *Weltanschauung*. Those myths, and what they entailed, were agents of socialization, the building blocks that created our sense of belonging.

In 1956 I was serving in the communication platoon of a combat unit in the IDF as part of my military duty. During the Sinai War (which was called 'Operation Kadesh') I saw Egyptian soldiers, barefoot, helpless, weaponless, coming down the scorching dunes of the Sinai desert, their hands held up, their tongues blackened from thirst. I watched how soldiers in my regiment forced them to drink urine and crawl on all fours towards the water canteens, then shoot them 'like dogs'. I saw violence and death become a pastime. Those were reserve soldiers, veterans of the Palmach and the Hagana (pre-state paramilitary organizations), upon which the myth of high moral standards and purity of weapons was erected. The myth shattered before my eyes.

Another myth, the one claiming that we fight only to defend ourselves against enemies intent on our annihilation, disintegrated when I realized that the Sinai War was not a defensive war but the result of an Israeli–Western initiative, motivated by political interests. In Israel there was no public debate about such matters, and the national myth-producing mechanism appropriated that war as a defensive one.

Confronted with these evils, I felt mute and isolated. I was confused and perplexed. Above all, I needed friends with whom I could think, discuss, clarify to myself what was right and wrong, and decide what course of action to take.

Years passed. Thoughts and feelings were slowly taking shape. I found friends who shared my convictions. They were few, outsiders mostly, who helped me break the silence and develop ideas and critical thinking. The overpowering loneliness and confusion I experienced at the beginning of my political involvement also taught me the strength and the comfort that members of affinity groups can bestow on each other.

Having seen Lamia, I realized that merely tending to his tortured body and soul could not make up for the anger and shame that I felt for being part of such a society. Thus the need arose to publicly expose the systematic – not the 'exception to the rule' – torture routinely carried out in the interrogation facilities of the Shabak (Israel's General

Security Services) and of the Israeli army: to openly and publicly campaign against torture.

I brought this suggestion before the Association of Israeli-Palestinian Physicians for Human Rights (PHR). The entire staff of the organization mobilized and for many months worked on preparing a public conference in Israel. The idea behind holding a conference on torture in Israel was the need to change the prevailing psycho-political perception in the common Israeli–Zionist society that maintains that protecting the 'insider' requires the elimination of the 'outsider'.

Freud once said: 'Men talk in order not to kill.' For many years the State of Israel declared that it would not talk with Palestinians, which in this context is tantamount to saying: They must be killed; we must use organized violence to suppress them.

The torture that the state uses against Palestinian 'outsiders' is a kind of mental superstructure of violence. The declared purpose of using torture is to force the enemy, the outsider, to talk and reveal secrets. This revelation is supposed to forestall the killing of insiders, members of the group. This way of reasoning is so facile and simplistic that it is readily and uncritically accepted. Presenting the issues in this manner provides validity and justification for torture.

But further examination of torture beyond this simplistic presentation exposes its speciousness. The victim's confession is useless. The torturer knows that the victim's words are worthless. A tormented person will tell the torturers what they want to hear – empty, mute speech, which does not accomplish the declared purpose of revealing secrets. In fact, the real purpose of torture is silence: silence induced by fear. Fear is contagious and spreads to the other members of the oppressed group, to silence and paralyse them. To impose silence through violence is torture's real purpose, in the most profound and fundamental sense.

The task of those who fight torture and organized violence is to speak for those who are silenced, to give voice to the muted shouts of fear and pain, to speak out and break down the walls of silence that shield the tormentors and their collaborators.

While organizing the conference and deciding on its basic conception, we were beset by many questions and dilemmas, such as: Where should we hold the conference? In the Occupied Territories? In Israel? If in Israel, should it be in Jerusalem, which is burdened with religious and political conflicts? Or perhaps in Tel Aviv, the most 'Israeli' city, the pulsating heart of the Israeli–Zionist society? Who is our target audience? Physicians? Human rights organizations? The general public?

Should we invite speakers who will argue for the need for torture? Is there justification, from our point of view, in allowing them to bring their case before the public? Should we invite members of the Knesset (the Israeli parliament)? And if so, should they be representatives of the political right, the left or perhaps the centre?

Should we publicly expose and condemn individual physicians whom we knew had given false medical statements so as to cover up the infliction of torture practised by Israeli interrogators? Or would it be both fairer and more effective to address the fundamental issue of doctors' collaboration in acts of torture? Such collaboration stems mostly from political obtuseness and unwillingness to understand the consequences of their acts, but also from the fact that there are no existing, accessible mechanisms for doctors to report instances of torture which come to their attention or which they themselves treat.

The answers to these questions are found in this book.

The struggle is by nature long and continuous. Campaigning against torture in a country like Israel must entail more than condemnation and exposure. In order for it to be effective, we must strive to create a cohesive public position that will counterbalance the primal myths of the group. In a society where camaraderie among soldiers is of paramount importance, to talk of torture is tantamount to state treason. The campaign against torture in Israel must, therefore, strive to create a different kind of cohesive force, one based on respect for the human body and the human spirit, and for moral values which transcend those of the tribe.

People all around the world who fight against torture and other forms of organized violence – human rights organizations both in Israel and elsewhere – are the answer, the source of support and encouragement, for men and women who feel shame and anger at the sight of torture.

As these words are being written, the agreement between Israel and the Palestine Liberation Organization (PLO) has already been signed, and the administration of Gaza and Jericho is gradually to be handed over to the Palestinian Authority. However, our work at the Association of Israeli-Palestinian Physicians for Human Rights indicates no decrease in human rights violations since the signing of the agreement in September 1993.

Indeed, about one million Palestinians still live under Israeli occupation in the West Bank, where the level of organized violence has not diminished. Additionally, a review of the agreement between Israel and the PLO reveals no provisions for the safeguarding of human rights. We are concerned about the situation on both sides of the border.

In Israel, Sheikh Durani, who was abducted in Lebanon, is being held in prison, while access to information about the conditions of his interrogation is denied to both Israeli and international human rights organizations. In Gaza, a Palestinian prisoner died under interrogation by the Palestinian Secret Service soon after the arrival of the Palestinian police there.

It is clear that the struggle against torture must go on. This book is intended as a tool for individuals or groups who oppose organized violence, cruel punishments, humiliations and the physical and mental abuse of people wherever they are carried on.

I hope that it will contribute to their struggle against it.

Tel Aviv
August 1994

PART I

The public realm

2 Associations

DAHLIA RABIKOVITCH

What has she got to say?
What has she got to say?
What else has she got to say?
She has a perverse craving for anguish.
And in our country the landscape is pretty,
Vineyards hang from the mountain side,
The shadow of clouds upon the plane
And sunlight
And a fenced plot;
As well as three rows of olive trees
That were uprooted in retribution.
And three old women with teeth extracted.
From old age, what else?
Violence doesn't prevail everywhere.
Why suddenly into that clear Sabbath
That felicitous Sabbath,
Sneaks the memory of this man beaten to death.
Him and his son thou shall not put to death on one day.

The stain of a light cloud
Has settled upon the plane.
In Zichron Yaacov[1] the cellar is bursting
With grapes' nectar.
Also our granaries have filled up with corn
And the valleys with plenty of water,
And under the overturned stone
A scorpion is crawling.
Nature's hymn.
And this Arab there they had beaten to death.
Literally smashed his body beating him.
But neither in Zichron Yaacov
Nor in Mazkeret Batya.[2]
Those are the Baron's colonies,
Sleepy, merging with the landscape.

What has she got to say?
What has she got to say?
She is just looking everywhere for pain
And for something to resent.
She is not one of us,
She does not see all the good and beauty in life.
She does not see us for what we are.
We returned to our homeland.

1992

Notes

1. Zichron Yaacov literally translated means 'the memory of Jacob'. It is the name of one of the early Jewish settlements supported by Baron Rothschild.

2. Mazkeret Batya translates as 'Batya's souvenir' and is another of the early settlements.

Poem translated by Yael Nir.

3 Political evil: legalized and concealed sadism

HAIM GORDON

We are living in a period of Israeli oppression of a Palestinian uprising. The Palestinian people want to live in freedom. Israel so far has refused to grant that freedom, and continues to oppress the Palestinians brutally. What is more, much sadism emerges in Israel's continual oppression of the Palestinian uprising, especially, but not only, in the interrogations of Palestinian suspects by the Israeli Security Services. I want briefly to examine the legitimization of this sadism within Israeli society.

How does sadism and the inflicting of undue suffering upon Palestinians become both acceptable and legal, as it is in Israel? How is this brutal everyday act of physically debasing another human being, of engaging in political evil, linked to the way of life of the sadist? Why do liberals and human rights activists fail to halt such blatant instances of political evil? In what follows I shall attempt a partial answer to these questions.

The history of the twentieth century reveals that the instigators of political evil are often very clever, and insidious. Again and again they distance themselves from sadism. They aspire to be thought of as normal – perhaps at times as cruel or brutal, but never as sadists. They repeatedly attempt to convey the message: If sadism emerges in their regime while they pursue their urgent political programme and their legitimate aims, it is only on the fringes. It is an 'unfortunate' aberration. Furthermore, one immediately apprehends that they do not reject sadism for what it is - the delight in dehumanizing other human beings, the joy in the gross infliction of undue suffering upon a free individual. No. Today's evil political leaders outwardly reject sadism for pragmatic reasons. For them sadism is not wrong or evil; it is an approach that can endanger the realization of political goals.

One can already grasp a major reason for this supposed abhorrence of sadism. Even evil political leaders in the twentieth century know that usually civilized people do not enjoy seeing or hearing about the joy of torturing, except perhaps if these are imaginary torturings, such as those depicted on television or at the cinema. The delights of inflicting physical suffering portrayed in detail by the Marquis de Sade do not thrive unquestioned in what is called 'respectable society', and probably thrive even less in the public space. In short, twentieth-century instigators of political evil know that the joy some people attain through inflicting horrible sufferings upon contemporary Justines must be very well concealed, or camouflaged.

Let me say it again. Sadism is not respectable. It can cause scandals, it can arouse the abhorrence of one's political supporters, and the twentieth-century instigators of political evil know this. They also know that if they are acknowledged as respectable it will greatly help them to conceal any evil doings attributed to them or to their regime. But these instigators of political evil do face problems. They frequently need to use brutal and violent means to attain some of their political goals. Furthermore, it would be best if this cruelty and violence were kept secret.

Enter the sadist. He or she fits the bill perfectly. Let me formulate this simple truth: The political goals of evil politicians and of evil regimes are often best attained by giving full rein and unqualified support to acknowledged sadists. One reason for this is that the politicians in these regimes know that the sadists will brutally and cruelly debase human beings with delight, and that they will rarely disclose their sadistic inclinations or their vile deeds to members of respectable society. Here is where, in totalitarian regimes, the evil sadism of the likes of Dr Mengele can find their niche. This point requires further elaboration.

Learning from Hannah Arendt's discussion of totalitarianism, it is clear that Dr Mengele's experiments on human beings were merely a logical extension of the major political goal of Nazi totalitarianism: the complete annihilation of political freedom and of the public space needed for it to come into being. Less extreme than Dr Mengele, but in full accordance with Nazi political goals, was the sadism of many of the officials in the Nazi death camps; this sadism was deemed necessary for running these camps, which were full-scale experiments in the annihilation of the public space that is necessary for freedom to emerge. Also less extreme, in most cases, was the sadism of the Cheka investigators and of the guards in Stalin's Gulag Archipelago, as portrayed in some detail by Alexander Solzhenitsyn and other Soviet writers. Yet one fact unites all these instances of sadism. The political regime used sadists to fulfil its political goals, yet it did everything in its power to conceal the existence of sadism in its camps and jails from the world outside those camps and jails.

In a democratic regime sadism is often outlawed. It is publicly recognized as repugnant, or even as a crime. It is a scandal when practised by officials representing the government. When sadistic deeds are disclosed, people readily declare their abhorrence of brutality and their anger at someone's delight or sexual satisfaction that has been obtained by brutally beating and violating another person. The recently aired videotape which filmed four members of the Los Angeles Police Department brutally beating, for no apparent reason, Rodney King, an Afro-American suspect whom they had just arrested, aroused much initial public rage in Los Angeles and across the United States. When the police officers were acquitted of all wrongdoing, the rage of the residents of south-central Los Angeles spilled onto the streets in unprecedented rioting. Even while condemning the riots in Los Angeles, many people in the United States were appalled at the acquittal of the policemen for their blatant sadistic acts, such as seen on the videotape.

Yet in Israel, and in other so-called democratic countries, laws have been passed that allow sadists to perform deeds that accord with the political evil that the regime initiates and strives to fulfil. This sadism, however, is usually performed incognito and behind closed doors. Often, if and when it leaks out, it is regarded as an exceptional case or as justified by the urgent needs of state security. Yet in order to understand how such sadism interacts with the political evil of the regime, it is important to describe in some detail the existential stance adopted by those sadists who serve the government, and by those governments that sanction or legalize sadism. How does this existential stance differ from a stance based on justice?

One of the underlying demands of any judical procedure or any theory of justice is that guilt has to be proven. It is a truism that the major reason for the demand that guilt must be proven is that innocence, as such, can never be proven. The Bible mentions what twentieth-century psychologists have repeatedly disclosed: every person has, at times, evil intentions and evil fantasies. Hence, to prove one's innocence is well nigh impossible. Nor is it the issue in judical procedures. All one needs to do is to show that one is not guilty. But even that is an exaggeration. The onus of proof is strictly on the prosecutor. He or she must present to the court facts that clearly prove the guilt of the accused. And the accused can choose to be silent during the entire procedure; at least, that is his or her full legitimate right in most non-totalitarian regimes. Neither the prosecutor nor the interrogator has any right to force the accused to speak. Thus, in a just juridical procedure, the need to prove that one is innocent never occurs. It does not need to; it is irrelevant to the entire procedure.

Totalitarian regimes changed all this. In Nazi Germany, Jews were born guilty; they were vile by virtue of their ancestry, guilty by birth of being the unwanted scum of the earth. Furthermore, every German had to prove his or her innocence from such guilt by showing that he or she had no Jewish ancestors for at least three generations. In the Soviet Union under Stalin, one was much more secure if one had no members of the bourgeoisie or nobility among one's ancestors. These approaches arouse a profound sense of horror at what vice-laden regimes can do. Nevertheless, they are instructive. They can help us outline the existential stance and the broadly held justifications, presented by totalitarian leaders, which allow the basic assumption that a person does not need to prove their innocence to be discarded.

This existential stance demands that one discard the value of each individual human being. It requires the development of a profound disrespect for the freedom and uniqueness of one's fellow man or woman. And more important in our context, it entails disregarding the wisdom of centuries as to what constitutes a just juridical procedure. Perhaps most important, this totalitarian stance requires the so-called 'security of the state', 'vitality of the race' or 'consciousness of the class' – whatever these phrases mean! – to be perceived as one's overruling concern. Indeed, in all totalitarian regimes it is stated that such concerns justify oppression, exploitation and mass murders. They also justify the brutal torture of so-called enemies of the regime so as to extract confessions from them that may be used in kangaroo courts. In the process of adopting such a stance and practising these atrocities, human beings discard the notion that guilt has to be proven.

Despite the fact that democracies differ greatly from totalitarian regimes, it is not inconceivable that the same existential stance may prevail in what are called democratic states. In these states, however, it is primarily the so-called 'security of the state' that justifies the adoption of a totalitarian stance and the practice of state-sanctioned evil. This evil usually includes the blatant oppression and destruction of human freedom, blended with disdain and scorn for the basic assumptions underlying a just juridical process. Furthermore, this stance and justification allow state-sanctioned sadism to flourish in democracies incognito.

Consider an Israeli Security Services interrogator of Palestinians in any of the Israeli prisons for Palestinians. (All interrogators are males and volunteer for this well-paid job.) The definition of the interrogator's job or vocation is not to gather information that will help to prove the guilt of any of the Palestinians whom he is interrogating. From dozens of personal interviews with Palestinians who had been interrogated, I can categorically state that the idea that a person is innocent until proven guilty, and that one needs well-supported facts to prove that a person is indeed guilty, never – but never – concerns the Israeli interrogator. Nor does it concern his superiors in the Security Services, nor most of the elected politicians whose role is to oversee the workings of the Security Services. Besides, the interrogator never respects the right of the suspected Palestinian to be silent and to refuse to answer questions. The interrogator has only one role: cruelly to use brute physical force, threats and, at times, cleverly woven lies to extract confessions from tortured Palestinians. He seldom cares if the deed that a Palestinian confesses to having done had really been committed by him or her.

The interrogator's role defines his existential stance. He voluntarily performs political evil. He beats up, tortures and violently abuses Palestinians daily. Many of these interrogators attain great satisfaction and much physical and perhaps even sexual gratification when their brutality has results; the Palestinian signs a document 'confessing' to, say, throwing a Molotov cocktail at Israeli soldiers. Their gratification is not only from the bodily act of beating, but from the fact that while relating to the Palestinian as an abject object they allowed him or her to retain enough freedom so as to confess. As Sartre has pointed out, this duality in the relationship of the interrogator towards the Palestinian that he is torturing – on the one hand, seeing the Palestinian as an abject object not worthy of human respect, and hence warranting brutal torture, and at the same time viewing the Palestinian as a free human being whose confession is an expression of that freedom and can be presented in court – this duality is of the essence of sadism. Because no sadist would want to beat a mere abject object: rather, what fascinates the sadist, what arouses his or her delight and sexual gratification, is that this person whom one brutally beats, as if he or she were an abject object, has the freedom to respond to one's beatings.

Thus, sadism, in which the interrogator attains much personal and physical gratification from brutally beating the Palestinians, is part of his vocation. How could it be otherwise? Once one has entered into the role of a torturer, as writers from the Marquis de Sade to Jean Genet have repeatedly shown, one has initiated a dialectical process whereby one's body which is doing the beating feels gratified – often sexually – when the torture leads to the desired result. Thus, for the Israeli interrogator the torture he inflicts upon Palestinians is not only justified by its results; these results also lend legitimacy to the pleasure and gratification that he often feels while torturing his prisoner. In short, the means and the end have changed roles. At first, perhaps, some interrogators torture Palestinians so as to attain a confession. Later, they attain a confession so as to justify their satisfaction in inflicting torture. And later still, as many examples I have recorded reveal, no justifications are needed. They beat up Palestinians for the gratification of inflicting pain and for the joy that wells up in one's being when one knows that another person, endowed originally with freedom, is totally in one's power, and one can express that power by making that person suffer.

Someone may ask here: Do you mean to say that all such Israeli interrogators are state-sanctioned committed sadists? I would answer: Yes. The dialectical process of beating and torturing which they initiate with every interrogation of a Palestinian leads them to nurture and to develop their sadistic inclinations. Such a dialectical development is hardly novel, especially if we note that the Israeli interrogator has a clean conscience since he is employed by the supposedly democratic State of Israel. He partakes in the legal judical process sanctioned by that state. His goal, yes, his only goal, is to attain confessions.

Of course, an Israeli interrogator can justify, say, his violent beatings of a tied prisoner by citing 'security of the state'. But even these justifications are banal and paltry when one considers the amount of undue torture that the Palestinians undergo. Yet, I do want to emphasize again that what occurs in Israel is just an example of the state-sanctioned sadism that thrives in a number of so-called democracies. Colombia and El Salvador come to mind. The details of this sanctioned-sadism are often seemingly hidden behind a wall of secrecy. But, at least in Israel, whoever wishes to know more about state-sanctioned sadism can quite easily get the information. I suspect that this is true in other countries also. Hence, a problem arises; if the facts concerning state-sanctioned sadism are available, and if many people intuitively abhor sadism, why do these people allow such political evil to continue?

One source of explanation may be found in the Landau Report, which followed an investigation of the methods of the Israel Security Services initiated by the Israeli government. In the report, the retired supreme court justice Moshe Landau, who headed the investigating commission, and his associates reached the conclusion that 'moderate physical pressure' is legitimate when interrogating Palestinians.

I feel no need to explain in detail why the Landau Report, which permits torture under the heading of 'moderate physical pressure', is a document that sanctions political evil. Nor does one need to explain that in submitting such a report and suggesting that it become the law of the land Justice Landau and his commission members were evildoers.

But I do want to emphasize that in the wake of the Landau Commission's pernicious recommendations, Israeli interrogators are now acting according to law when they daily torture Palestinian prisoners. Of course, all this arouses associations with what has been published about torture under totalitarian regimes – especially since Justice Landau and the members of his commission, and the government of Israel, citing as a reason 'the security of Israel', keep secret the exact methods of 'moderate physical pressure' which the report allows. If the physical pressure is moderate, justified and acceptable in terms of justice, why not describe it in detail? After hearing what some Palestinians underwent at the hands of the Israeli Security Services, I can state categorically that the methods of torture sanctioned by Justice Landau and concealed from the Israeli public are not at all moderate. Therefore, the cynical response of one Israeli Knesset member to Judge Landau's recommendations is quite accurate: At what voltage does an electric current applied to one's testicles stop being 'moderate physical pressure'?

One further important point should be made concerning the Landau Report. What concerned the Landau Commission was not that innocent people were being tortured, but rather that this torture was kept secret from the courts. They stated that they were appalled that members of the Israeli Security Service had for decades lied in court as to the methods they used to extract confessions from suspects. But their being appalled did not lead them to demand that justice be done and that the liars or the instigators of this policy be put on trial. Rather, they recommended that the matter be allowed to rest. The recommendation was accepted. The issue here is that damage to the façade of justice, through lies, concerned the Landau Commission much more than the beatings and sufferings and false condemnations of many innocent Palestinians and of other suspects. According to Moshe Landau and his commission, to brutally torture and physically abuse Palestinian prisoners is permissible – just don't lie about it in court!

Thus, the Landau Report, which became Israeli law, shows that Israel's system of interrogation, at least in relation to Palestinians, is based on a total disregard for human rights and civil rights. Worse, it tramples on the basic concept of juridical justice by ignoring the wisdom of centuries concerning guilt: A person is innocent until proven guilty; no accused person is required to speak out in response to the accusations; hence, guilt must be proven by facts, not by torturing a person until he or she confess. Furthermore, the Landau Report allows state-sanctioned sadism to don the mantle of legitimacy.

One of the greatest dangers of this report is that it makes state-sanctioned torture respectable. For those elements in Israeli society who call themselves 'nationalists', and who do not respect human rights, such legitimization of torture is a victory. This victory was enhanced by the fact that after the Landau Report became law many liberal lawyers and many other human rights activists hesitated to criticize it, to denounce Judge Landau and members of his commission, or to firmly denounce the torture of Palestinians in Israeli jails. They seem to have feared the response to such criticizm, that they might be branded traitors to the security needs of the Israeli state, or challengers of laws that were democratically passed in the Israeli Knesset. Put otherwise, today in Israel, few – very few – dare to challenge the sadistic activities of Israeli interrogators of Palestinians.

Consider the case of those Israeli medical doctors (all of them are males) who serve in the prisons where interrogation and torture of Palestinians take place daily. Each such prison has at least one doctor in service at all hours. His role is to examine beaten prisoners and to see if they can continue to be tortured; and at times his role is to heal them to a level of health that will allow the torture to continue. By working hand in glove with the interrogators who brutally beat and torture the Palestinians, and without denouncing torture, these Israeli doctors are silent accomplices in this crime. They are participants in this unjustifiable physical degradation of Palestinians. If they ever experienced horror at the terrible torture of fellow human beings, they have silenced their qualms. In addition, they are blatantly betraying their Hippocratic oath.

One probable reason for the fact that so many doctors willingly participate in allowing torture to be conducted is that, with the help of the Landau Report, sadism in Israel has been sanctioned by the state. Still, the participation of doctors in such torture is instructive, because the accepted social role of doctors has always been to heal the body and to alleviate pain. These prison doctors do the opposite. They participate in inflicting pain and in the destruction of the bodies of Palestinians who were being interrogated. Hence, the doctors who work with the torturers have chosen to betray the essence of their role and daily to participate in political evil. Such is perhaps the most vivid example of how, in Israel, state-sanctioned sadism supported by law has encouraged doctors to destroy some of their most basic humanitarian impulses and approaches. Such a destruction of humanistic approaches occurs also among the soldiers who guard the Palestinian prisoners. But these soldiers never undertook the role of healers and alleviators of pain, while the doctors who help the interrogators vowed to do exactly that.

While we consider legalized sadism in Israel, it should not be forgotten for a moment that sadism and the negation of humanitarian approaches in prisons, often with the assistance of medical doctors, also occur in many other so-called democratic countries – for instance, in Central America, in Egypt, in Turkey and in South Africa during the brutal reign of apartheid.

In summary, I want to stress one crucial point. The unwillingness of liberals, doctors and even human rights agencies to straightforwardly challenge and to firmly denounce state-sanctioned sadism often allows it to continue unabated. I hope that such a firm denunciation will emerge from this important conference.

4 The social response to torture in Israel

STANLEY COHEN

Allow me to begin by making two assumptions which would be widely accepted by those whose work concerns the observation of interrogation practices in Israel.

First, the torture and ill-treatment of Palestinian detainees under interrogation by various Israeli authorities has been routine, systematic and institutionalized for at least the last five years. Each year at least 6,000 detainees have experienced some form of treatment which I would call 'low-intensity torture' and which constitutes a violation of international human rights law.

Second, this ill-treatment of Palestinians at the hands of the Israeli authorities is well known to the vast majority of politically influential members of Israeli society. They might not be aware of the specific details, such as the legal framework or the jurisprudential arguments, but they are certainly aware of the general picture. There are, as we will see, some ambiguities concerning the use of the concept 'to know' in this context; but for members of this informed, newspaper-reading audience, it will simply not be possible in the years to come, when historians research our times, to use those terrible words 'we didn't know', 'no one told us', 'it couldn't have happened without us knowing', or 'it could have happened without us knowing'.

My question is, what happens to this knowledge? I will concentrate on the reactions of those two sections of Israeli society that are actively called upon to react: first, those in power, in official government circles, decision-makers, spokesmen and supporters (and here there are no real differences between the two major parties, Likud and Labour); and second, the group that I will call 'Meretz liberals'[1] – those who see themselves as the Israeli representatives of enlightened, democratic, 'Western' and liberal values.

I will not say much about the rest, the majority, of the population whose reaction is quite simply not to react. They are not called upon to take a position – nobody ever asks them what they think – and we must assume that their silence indicates a passive acquiescence. They are exercising their basic human right: what Daniel Ellsberg calls 'the right not to know'. Their reaction is captured in the wonderful Israeli expression 'lo echpad li', or in English, 'I don't give a damn'.

The authorities

Let me begin with the official government response. Here there is no real difference from what appeared in the text of the original Landau Commission Report in 1987. There is very little difference from what appears all over the world when governments (especially accountable governments) have to respond to allegations of torture or other gross human rights violations. Whether it is the Turkish government against the Kurds or the Indian government against the Kashmiris today, or the Argentinian government against their internal opponents a decade ago, or the French in Algeria forty years ago, the response is pretty much the same. It is almost as if there is a deep structure, a common vocabulary, which governments could be borrowing from each other. There are three fixed components to the response.

'Nothing is happening'

The first component is a complete and literal denial of the facts. All allegations and evidence are dismissed as lies, fabrications, fantasies or deliberate disinformation. Journalists who have been interviewing government officials in the last few days about the subject of this conference have been routinely told: 'It's all lies. You have been deceived. Only gullible foreign journalists believe these stories from over-imaginative Arabs or from the Israeli left. There is no torture in Israel. How could there be if we have ratified the Convention against Torture? It's not happening; nothing is happening.'

'What is happening is really something else'

Second, the facts are admitted (something is indeed happening) but their meaning is denied, reinterpreted or reallocated. This is often a question of semantics, or word games. The actual word 'torture' is avoided, and appropriate terms are developed in its place, what the Landau Commission called 'moderate physical pressure' or what the French in Algeria termed 'special procedures'. There are many other examples of such administrative euphemism or legal jargon.

'What is happening is completely justified'

Third, the procedures followed by the state are defended on the basis of extraordinary circumstances. Harsh procedures are deemed necessary to fight the war against terrorism (or communism, crime, fundamentalism or whatever); to preserve national security; to assist in intelligence gathering, extracting confessions, cracking Hamas cells, etc. The defence of necessity as a moral and legal justification for torture is, of course, as old as the phenomenon itself. No government in history has ever justified torture by saying that they 'like' doing it; torture always has to be justified in instrumental, utilitarian terms ('necessity').

When I first began to work on the issue of torture a few years ago, I tried hard to puzzle out the contradictory relationships between these three components. How was it possible that the same government official, the same judicial commission, the same editorial, could simultaneously say things which appeared to be so patently irreconcilable? How does one claim that 'nothing is happening' while simultaneously maintaining that 'what is happening is justified'? I came to realize that the puzzle only exists if you see these elements as separate and logically contradictory. In fact, they are politically dependent on each other. There is a fixed official discourse of torture (and other gross violations of human rights); these three elements always complement each other.

Torture victims themselves are all too familiar with this. They must struggle on two levels: first, against the official response which dismisses their claims to have been tortured as unfounded; and second, against the official claim that they have committed such terrible acts that they merely received what they deserved. This struggle starts from the moment that the interrogator says those terrible words: 'Scream as much as you like. No one will believe you when you come out'. And afterwards you are indeed not fully believed – and you are also regarded as guilty ('They must have done something'). In the classic response to allegations of atrocities committed during the Vietnam War: 'They're all lying and anyway the bastards got what they deserved.'

In addition to this fixed three-stage sequence, there are a number of other common official deflections which are shared by a wider circle, even the liberal community. These include:

— 'It's worse elsewhere' (Syria, Iraq …).
— 'Why does the world just pay attention to us?'
— 'They use a double standard against us.'
— 'Look at the violence they inflict on each other.'
— 'We always strictly follow the law.'
— 'Yes, there used to be abuses in the past, but the situation is now completely changed.'
— 'The abuses are extreme and deviant cases – and the offenders are strictly dealt with.'

Appropriate variations on these techniques of deflection are virtually universal and not specific to Israel. What I believe to be unique to Israel is the peculiarly Israeli form of self-righteous kitsch which asserts not only that what we are doing is also being done by everyone else, but that we are actually behaving in a better, more moral way than anyone else. The Landau Report, for example, insists that the use of moderate physical pressure is a humane policy, a deliberate way to preserve the suspect's 'human dignity'. Tying someone up, hooding them with a stinking sack, confining them in a closet, depriving them of sleep and beating them come to represent morally sensitive actions which make us superior to other nations facing similar conflicts.

There is another, more routine official response which is characteristic of the present Israeli government. The cliché offered to journalists and visitors enquiring about the subject of torture (for example by Yossi Beilin, the Deputy Foreign Minister who is responsible for human rights contacts) goes like this: 'There is no such thing as a benign occupation; nothing will change until there is a political solution; in the meantime some abuses will – regrettably – continue; indeed, to hasten a political solution, these abuses might even be necessary.' This line, of course, is more stupid and hypocritical than a simple ideological defence – and completely misses the point that human rights violations can never be justified by appeals to political expediency. This is exactly how the mass deportations in December 1992 came to be defended and precisely what the international human rights community has been working to condemn for fifty years.

The liberals

Let me now address the second source of response which is provided by that group which I refer to as 'Meretz liberals'. Of course, there are some honourable exceptions and many in this group have been firm, consistent and vocal on human rights issues. But on the whole, some qualifying prefix is needed to understand the peculiarly compromised nature of Israeli liberalism. Liberals here are not quite what they are elsewhere.

In most of the democratic world, torture is a quintessentially mainstream liberal issue. There is nothing 'radical' or 'extremist' in the international struggle against torture associated with organizations like Amnesty International. But in Israel, the identifiably liberal sectors of the community play no active part in the campaign against torture. The Israeli Bar Association, for example, has been totally silent. The only serious opposition comes from more 'radical' and marginal groups (like the two organizations responsible for staging this conference). The liberal discourse in Israel is much closer to the official government position than it should be.

There are, of course, some important differences. First, these liberals cannot and do not say that 'nothing is happening'. They admit the facts readily enough – they write about them in their newspapers, plays and poems; they make films and TV documentaries about them. There is, in fact, a large culture devoted to talking about human rights violations. Second, these groups are genuinely – if only privately – uncomfortable with their knowledge. Unlike the fake 'regrets' of government apologists, there is a real sense of moral and psychological unease.

What do people do when they know something but feel that they really do not want to have this knowledge or do not know what to do about it? Or when they cannot face its full implications? They do what we all do; we decide – sometimes more, sometimes less, consciously – that there are certain subjects that it would be better not to know too much about. How often do we all say, 'I don't really want to know about that'?

This process is nicely conveyed in a recent reinterpretation of the Oedipus legend by the British psychiatrist John Steiner. The conventional interpretation of the story is one of a quest for truth. At first, Oedipus does not know the facts – that he has killed his father, that he has had sexual relations with his mother – but gradually through the drama the awful truth is revealed. This is understood as a parable for psychotherapy itself; the patient, together with his or her analyst, comes to self-knowledge through the painful process of uncovering the truth.

Steiner suggests that a different interpretation of the legend is possible. Sophocles leaves us enough clues to show that Oedipus, as well as the other main characters of the story – the courtiers (or 'government officials' as we would refer to them today) – must have known the truth all along. They would have been real schmucks not to have known or at least guessed something of what had happened. But everyone had his or her own interest not to know, to evade the truth. The Oedipus legend then is not about the revelation of truth, but the suppression of truth. The legend is a cover-up story, like Watergate or Iran–Contra. Therefore the question is: how much did Nixon or Reagan or Bush really 'know'? The ambiguous means by which we avoid knowing too much about what we know is well conveyed in the everyday phrase which is the title of Steiner's paper: 'Turning a Blind Eye'.

When called upon to react, when someone insistently focuses the eye, these liberals can draw on some of the universal techniques of deflection: 'It's worse elsewhere' (and, in the case of torture, this is true; the Israeli methods are indeed 'moderate'); 'Everyone is picking on us' (which is also sometimes true). Then there are some special techniques – notably the liberal version of the Yossi Beilin line: Regrettably, these things will happen as long as there is no political solution. Therefore we have to support the security services (and policies such as the mass deportation and the closure of the Occupied Territories) as an unfortunate price to pay for some future peace. In fact, the tougher we are now, the easier it will be to make concessions in Washington.

There is yet another special twist in the rhetoric of Israeli liberals. After giving all of their reasons for their lack of active engagement, they will then assure you: 'We are so pleased that there are organizations like B'Tselem doing such a wonderful job. This shows how healthy Israeli democracy is.' When my colleague Daphna Golan and I wrote our report for B'Tselem on the subject of torture, people would tell us: 'Kol hakavod (congratulations). It's so good that people like you are doing this.'

Variations of these reactions are, of course, to be found elsewhere in the world. But again, I want to stress the particularly Israeli context. Most important here is the absence of any real fear of speaking out. Israeli democracy, in contrast to most regimes under which human rights violations take place, offers its citizens (Jewish citizens especially) enormous protection. The contours of civil liberties are more or less intact: freedom of speech and assembly, academic freedom, the absence of gross censorship. The major inhibition that exists to speaking out in other societies – the fear that you will be next in line, that you will be punished yourself, therefore it is prudent to keep silent – simply does not exist here. What has to be confronted here is the self-imposed silence, the internal inhibitions which prevent people from openly speaking about what they know. George Orwell expressed this nicely many years ago: 'Circus dogs jump when the trainer cracks his whip, but the really well trained dog is one that turns his somersault when there is no whip.'

To know and what's more to act

The motto of this conference is 'To know and what's more to act'. What can be done about those barriers which prevent private knowledge from being translated into public talk and action?

Obviously, we must continue to write reports and articles, do research, document stories, collect evidence and organize conferences like this. But for the reasons I have tried to set out, I doubt that the mere accumulation of more information is going to make much difference at this stage. Neither will new laws in themselves be enough without a supportive culture to enforce them.

What we ought to do is work to create a climate – a language, an opportunity, a set of procedures – to encourage people to speak out about what they know. I do not mean the General Security Services agents themselves (they are 'just doing their jobs') but the wider circles who are being absorbed and co-opted into their network of secrecy: the soldiers who escort detainees to interrogation wings; the doctors who fill out the forms certifying suspects as being 'fit' to be hooded and tied up; the lawyers and the military court judges who routinely accept confessions that they know were obtained by force. These people collude with what is happening not because there is a threat to their lives or personal security if they refuse to cooperate, but first and foremost because non-compliance is simply beyond their imagination.

Our task is to facilitate non-compliance, to make it easier, even rewarding, for people to speak out and to 'blow the whistle'. One way to do this is to make the price of silence heavier than the price of non-compliance and public reporting. The price for silence should be pressure from the international community, especially the medical, legal and academic communities. This pressure should be fair, pressure that does not single out Israel for special attention (the torture problem exists and is worse elsewhere), but includes Israel in the same universe of moral judgement as applied to other places.

There is no longer any point in repeating the moral and legal arguments about why torture is evil. Guilt, some inner sense of moral responsibilty, is a rather poor form of social control compared to shame, that is, the knowledge or anticipation of condemnation from others. From the trained professional interrogators (the paid 'dirty workers') to the simplest frightened 19-year-old recruit patrolling the alleys of Gaza, the actors in this story do what they do because they know that they will not feel ashamed in front of their relevant audiences. They will not feel ashamed in front of their immediate superiors, nor the legal authorities if they come to trial, nor their friends and families, nor even their putative liberal critics. All of these observers allow them their rationalizations, allow them to use their techniques of denial, justification or evasion.

These observers in turn – the audiences of officials, authorities and critics – will continue to use their rationalizations and denials as long as the powers on which they are dependent do not make them feel ashamed. We know just who these powers are in the case of Israel. And we might remind ourselves in this context of the human rights records of the world's three largest per capita recipients of aid from the United States: Turkey, Egypt and Israel.

There are very few generalizations that hold up in criminology, the academic discipline in which I work; however, one reasonable generalization is that criminals are symbiotically bound to their audiences, those who have observed them and will judge them. This applies no less to crimes of the state (as we call 'human rights violations') than it does to the conventional crimes of every day. This is why 'reacting to torture' is part of the explanation of why torture happens in the first place.

Note

1. Before the 1992 elections three political parties on the Israeli left established a coalition called *Meretz*. The parties forming *Meretz* are known for their continuing struggle against the violation of human rights and for their claim that only a 'two-state solution' worked out with the Palestinians can lead to peace. After the elections they joined the Labour Party in order to establish a government that would pursue peace.

Suggested reading

B'Tselem (Israeli Information Centre for Human Rights in the Occupied Territories), *The Interrogation of Palestinians during the Intifada: Ill-Treatment, 'Moderate Physical Pressure' or Torture?*, Jerusalem, 1991.

B'Tselem, *The Interrogation of Palestinians during the Intifada: Follow-Up to March 1991 B'Tselem Report*, Jerusalem, 1992.

Cohen, Stanley, 'Talking about torture in Israel', *Tikkun*, vol. 6, November 1991.

Israel Law Review, vol. 23, no. 2, 1989, special issue on the Landau Report.

Landau Commission, *Report of the Commission of Enquiry into the Methods of Investigation of the General Security Services Regarding Hostile Terrorist Activity* (the Landau Report), Jerusalem, State of Israel, 1987.

Moderate Physical Pressure, Transcript of symposium organized by the Public Committee against Torture in Israel, Jerusalem, 1990.

Workshop: strategies for an international campaign against torture in Israel

led by JONATHAN E. FINE

The premise of the workshop was that international public opinion is a crucial determinant in the struggle to eliminate torture in Israel. The abhorrence of torture by the world public is virtually universal. Thus, most governments employing torture fear international awareness of its practice. International condemnation undermines a state's moral standing in the world community and threatens the availability of international assistance. Israel is no exception. Apparently immune for decades from these sanctions, Israel is coming under increasing scrutiny from within and without for the systematic employment of torture practices and for other serious abuses of human rights.

In order to mobilize public opinion, the participants concluded, intensified national and international campaigning is necessary. For such advocacy to function optimally, it must be coordinated effectively with existing Israeli and Palestinian organizations. Close and sustained cooperation between indigenous entities and their counterparts in the international community will strengthen the fact-finding and advocacy of both parties.

The participants agreed that torture investigations and campaigning should encompass the inclusive language of Article 5 of the Universal Declaration of Human Rights: 'No one shall be subjected to torture or to cruel, inhuman or degrading treatment or punishment.'

Proposals for Action

1 Effort should be made to ensure that human rights in general, and torture specifically, are on the agenda of negotiations in the peace process, for there will be no meaningful peace without respect for human rights and unless torture is eliminated.

2 Governments providing aid to Israel must be persuaded through international campaigning to make assistance conditional on the respect for human rights in the country.

3 A special effort should be made to mobilize support from Jewish communities in countries outside of Israel, without neglecting advocacy of non-Jewish communities and institutions. It is important

to make known the fact that there are Israelis who are critical of their government's systematic human rights abuses.

4 Professional bodies such as medical and bar associations should be mobilized to take action on individual cases of torture and other grave violations of the integrity and dignity of persons in detention. Professional bodies within Israel should be encouraged to request action by their counterparts internationally, and conversely, professional associations outside of Israel should be encouraged to develop regular communication with their Israeli counterparts on these cases.

5 Jewish and other religious leaders outside of Israel should be urged to request action by Israel's rabbis. The contradiction of the practice of torture by a 'Jewish state' must be emphasized in order to mobilize the political influence of this group in Israeli society.

6 Health professionals often come in contact with the victims of torture. This access gives them unique opportunities – and responsibilities – in the struggle against torture. Initiatives must be taken to gain support from national and international medical associations against violations of medical ethics committed by Israeli physicians who are either witnesses to, or participants in, torture or other inhumane and degrading practices. These appeals should be directed to the Israeli Medical Association, to health authorities within Israel and to other medical bodies outside of Israel and to the world community at large. As medicine is organized within Israel and internationally by specialist and subspecialist societies, these groups also must be appealed to for appropriate action.

Note

The workshop on international campaigning was attended by about forty individuals from several countries, who participated in an active exchange of views and opinions.

Participation of health professionals in the practice of torture: the struggle against it

5 The white coat passes like a shadow: the health profession and torture in Israel

RUCHAMA MARTON

> The doctor shall not countenance, condone or participate in the practice of torture or other forms of cruel, inhuman or degrading procedures, whatever the offence of which the victim of such procedures is suspected, accused or guilty, and whatever the victim's beliefs or motives, and in all situations, including armed conflict and civil strife.

World Medical Association, Declaration of Tokyo, 1975

The white coat passes like a shadow through the interrogation centres which include 'the coffin', 'the refrigerator', 'the banana knot' and the terrifying darkness of being hooded. The doctor is in the background, behind every torturer/interrogator. A doctor performs a pre-torture examination. He provides medical approval granting 'fitness for interrogation'. A doctor monitors the torture process. A doctor examines and takes care of the prisoner following the infliction of torture. A doctor writes a medical opinion or a pathologist's report.

Working in the Occupied Territories we see neglect, deprivation, destruction and bereavement. As physicians working in this conflict-plagued area, we have learned that the essential problem is not to heal the ill; rather, the fundamental challenge is to change what human beings are capable of doing to one another. The worst of these actions is the practice of torture.[1] The Israeli Medical Association (IMA) endorsed the World Medical Association's Declaration of Tokyo against torture (1975). Unfortunately, many Israeli doctors do not apparently meet the demands and duties of the Tokyo Declaration.

Of the many appeals made to the Association of Israeli-Palestinian Physicians for Human Rights (PHR), I will present you with two cases illustrating the manner in which the Shabak (Israel's General Security Services) practises torture, termed by the Landau Commission 'moderate physical pressure'.[2] The first case is that of Nader Raji Michael Kumsiah, 25 years old, from Beit Sachur.[3] He was arrested on the night of 3 May 1993 at his home and taken to the detention camp in Dahariah. Nine days later, on 12 May, Nader Kumsiah was brought before Judge Altbaur for the purpose of extending his detention.

According to the protocol of the hearing, Kumsiah denied the charges against him and told the judge: 'Yesterday and the day before I was tortured during investigation. They hit me on the testicles and took me to the hospital.' In his decision to extend detention, the judge wrote:

> the head of the interrogation center presented at my request a report from Soroka hospital, according to which the prisoner was hurt harshly in both of his testicles (a rupture) as a result of a blow. The commander of the detention facility notified the court that he is directing an investigation concerning the source of the blow, and I am directing the commander of the detention facility to bring forth the conclusion of this investigation before the judge that will determine whether or not to extend the detention of the prisoner.

On 19 May, Nader Kumsiah was brought before Judge Livni, who decided against extending detention on the grounds of a lack of evidence, but agreed that Kumsiah should be held in administrative detention. PHR was asked by Kumsiah's family to intervene in the case. In the investigation that PHR conducted, we discovered that Kumsiah's medical file containing the medical report quoted in Judge Altbaur's decision was missing from the Soroka Hospital archives. The only document given to the family was a medical opinion written on 19 May, eight days after Kumsiah's release from the emergency room. This medical opinion, signed by a urologist, reads: 'Nader reached the emergency room because of a rupture in the scrotal region. According to the patient, he had fallen down the stairs two to five days before he came to the diagnostic room.' Mr Kumsiah insists that he neither fell down the stairs nor ever said anything to this effect to anyone.[4]

This medical letter was written retroactively, without any further examination, and is inconsistent with the letter quoted by the judge. It seems to us that this letter was fabricated in an attempt to blur the facts. The physician makes no reference to the rupture in the patient's scrotum which had apparently resulted from a blow during interrogation, and tried to attribute the injury to 'falling down the stairs'. Can anyone imagine a person falling down the stairs and injuring his scrotum?

If the physician were obliged to report to the Israeli Medical Association (IMA) and the police, and if he had known that the IMA would support and encourage him to report an act of torture or other abuses, he might not have failed as, we feel, he did, and would not have been complicit in a crime of torture, which violates medical ethics and the Declaration of Tokyo.

The second example is a case of torture resulting in severe emotional and mental damage. Hassan Bader Abdallah Zbeidi, aged 34, is a university graduate, married and father to four children. He was arrested at his home on 25 September 1992 and brought to the Tulkarm detention camp. For twenty days his family did not know where he was. One month after his arrest, on 28 October, Hassan Zbeidi was released from detention without any charges having been filed against him.

'Released from detention' is a military euphemism. Actually, Hassan Zbeidi was taken to his home in a civilian automobile which soldiers had stopped at a road-block and ordered to 'bring him to his home'. He arrived home in a severely catatonic condition; he was unable to establish contact with the outside world. He recognized nobody, not his wife or children, nor his parents. He did not respond or talk spontaneously, and he was incontinent. He had an empty, frozen stare, and his body was stooped and shaking. He would remain frozen in the position in which he was placed.

What happened to Hassan Zbeidi in the interrogation wing operated by the Shabak in Tulkarm? While not able to find out for certain, we are able to speculate on an informed basis, because at the same time, in September and October 1992, we received five complaints of torture from Tulkarm Prison.[5] Recurring descriptions included blows to all parts of the body, blows to the testicles, being tied to a pipe, a sack on one's head, prolonged standing, and suffocation. One of these five prisoners, Mustafa Barakat, died while under interrogation in the same prison in Tulkarm. The others were released without being charged.

Hassan Zbeidi's experience is no exception; he is just another person who was severely tortured and returned to his home disabled, with little hope. I examined Hassan Zbeidi several times, and in cooperation with a Palestinian doctor from Nablus he received medication. His family is warm and supportive, and gradually there has been a slight improvement in his condition. When I examined Zbeidi in the spring of 1993, he had begun to speak a little. He answered questions slowly, in a very quiet voice, with long pauses. He said that he remembers being hit in the head and chest, that his head was slammed against the wall and that he was strangled. He also remembers waking up from the beating in the hospital.

Despite repeated denials and efforts to conceal the facts and documents, we were able to obtain a copy of the medical certification from the emergency room of Tel Hashomer Hospital from 4:07 p.m., 15 October 1992. The attending physician had written:

Main problem – recently quieter than normal. Memory disturbances. Doesn't complain about anything specific. According to the military doctor's report he is 'sad and disoriented as to location and time. Appears to be in convulsion.'

Relevant findings:

Calm, no pallor, cyanosis or jaundice.
Head & Neck – no pathological findings.
Lungs – clean.
Heart – clear voices.
Stomach – soft. Arms and Legs – no pathological findings.
Examination of Psychiatrist – No clearly defined problem.
Examination of emergency room Neurologist – normal. Impression that patient is malingering.

Observation:

1. Follow-up of prison physician.
2. Treatment with any placebo.
3. If condition worsens – send to doctor.

As far as we know, four doctors examined Hassan Zbeidi: the military doctor who referred him to the emergency room, the emergency room physician, a psychiatrist and a neurologist. Although Zbeidi was apparently suffering from a serious psychosis, not one of them raised his voice to protect him. For instance, the emergency room physicians appear to have ignored the clear and succinct language of the military doctor, which stated that Zbeidi 'is disoriented as to location and time'. These words, when used by a physician, are clearly indicative of a condition of psychosis. All three of the emergency room doctors ignored his serious condition, diagnosed him as a deceiver and gave him a placebo.

These doctors neither placed Zbeidi under medical supervision, nor reported to any authority that his injuries seemingly resulted from interrogation performed by the Shabak. They returned him to his interrogators, despite the fact that their diagnoses and recommendations exhibit comprehension of the gravity of his condition. This is further indicated by the third recommendation: 'If condition worsens – send to doctor.' The condition of a deceiver does not get worse, the condition of a patient can. These civilian doctors, who are not under military control, chose to cooperate with torturers of their own free will. In so doing, they betrayed the trust that was placed in them as physicians, on both ethical and medical levels. The IMA must issue clear guidelines obliging its member physicians to report incidents of torture. The application of such guidelines in hospital emergency rooms would help prevent conduct such as that of the doctors who returned Zbeidi – who went mad out of pain and terror – to his interrogators.

Here is an official form that the doctor fills out after examining a prisoner in an interrogation centre in Israel:

Dept of Interrogation
Form of Medical Fitness

No. of Prisoner _____ name _____ date _____

1. On _____ I examined the above prisoner and his medical findings are:
a. _____
b. _____
c. _____
d. _____
e. _____

2. As a result of the above, the medical limitations on the conditions of imprisonment are:
a. Are there any limitations to the prisoner's stay in an isolated cell. Yes/No
b. Are there any limitations to the prisoner's chaining? Yes/No
c. Are there any limitations to wearing head/eyes cover? Yes/No
d. Are there any limitations to prolonged standing? Yes/No
e. Does the prisoner have physical injuries (before entering interrogation)? Yes/No
f. Main medical limitation:
1) _____
2) _____
3) _____
4) _____

Doctor's signature_____

Notice that the form says: 'Does the prisoner have physical injuries (before entering interrogation)?' What are we to make of this? That now the one being investigated is prepared for sleep deprivation, starvation, exposure to intense heat, to freezing cold, to pain from blows, being tied in painful positions for long periods of time, being forced to stand for long periods, having one's head covered by a stinking and suffocating sack, being humiliated, sexual exploitation and having his spirit broken by prolonged solitary confinement?

A 'medical fitness form' certifies the person to be 'fit for interrogation', which leads to torture. The physician knows that he is providing his services – his agreement and approval – to a systematic process, the purpose of which is to break a person's soul and body.

Physicians could learn from the legal establishment's banning of evidence obtained through torture. Jurists, though not physicians, first published evidence in the early eighteenth century that there is no connection between pain and truth. They banned the use of torture for legal purposes and disqualified confessions obtained by inflicting pain or torture. One assumes that the heads of the Shabak, the Israeli army and the Israeli police are also aware of the spurious relationship between pain and truth. Nevertheless, torture and brutality are still practised, and physical and psychological 'pressure' are still applied.

Why do they do this? It would appear that they do so because the true objective of torture is to break the spirit of the person and to alter their personality. The judicial system necessitates a pragmatic approach. Before all else a physician should be committed to ethics and personal morality. Anything that causes a person physical or mental suffering is unacceptable to the medical profession. The most important statement of the Hippocratic oath is: 'Primum non nocere', which means 'Above all, do not harm', as a minimal demand that one must not transgress.

In all of these situations, the doctor is providing his services to the state, the regime, and not to the patient. The doctor who cooperates in the practice of torture is a partner in crime. Should the prisoner die during interrogation, the doctor is in fact assisting in murder. Doctors, nurses, medical assistants and judges who see and know yet cover up are all accomplices in a crime.

We must uncompromisingly oppose torture. As human beings we must oppose it with all our might, and a particular obligation rests on physicians. We, who live under a democratic regime, must act within the framework of democracy. In other words, we are obliged to refuse to cooperate in the committing of crimes against human beings.

When facing the fact that the State of Israel practises torture, Israeli society employs two defence mechanisms. The first is rationalization – a political argument – whereby the practice of torture is dismissed merely as a symptom of the Occupation; we console ourselves that, when the Occupation ends, so also will the practice of torture. However, torture is indicative of a world-view in which human rights have no value. Torture was practised before the Occupation, and there is no reason to believe that anything should change if the Occupation ever ceases, unless we manage to change our world-view, of which torture has become a part. We must not behave as though we are living under a dictatorial regime which may torture and kill whoever is not a collaborator. The essence of a democracy is that the person is above the regime, and the doctor's profession binds him ethically to this principle.

The other defence mechanism is denial. Many Israelis think that torture belongs to another place or another time – in World War II, in South America – but not here and now. It is painful for Israelis to think that there are torture cells in the State of Israel. This is why so many Israeli Jews are unable to allow themselves to know about it. One of the objectives of PHR is to make clear that torture, even if it is referred to with different terms, is being systematically practised in Israel. It is not an exceptional occurrence. We aim to disturb the peace of mind achieved through denial and ignorance which lead to passivity. We must involve the public in an active struggle against torture.

We would like to demonstrate that violent and cruel methods of interrogation cannot add to our security, even if they are practised for this purpose. Immoral norms fail to contribute to our personal safety, nor do they contribute to the security of the state as a whole. Instead, they lead to a vicious circle of social and personal disintegration.

If we citizens in general, and physicians specifically, do not ensure that it is forbidden to harm a person's body or soul through the practice of torture for any reason whatsoever, not even for the sake of the state's security, we will find ourselves directly or indirectly supporting the destruction of personal and social morality.

Epilogue

The Association of Israeli–Palestinian Physicians for Human Rights wrote a letter in June 1993 to the IMA protesting against the Security Services' use of the 'Form of Medical Fitness' and the evidence that it provides of complicity with torture being extended by physicians in the detention system. Dr Miriam Tzangen, Chairperson of the IMA, had been unaware of the existence of this form. She wrote an urgent letter to Prime Minister Yitzhak Rabin, declaring that doctors serving in prisons should refuse to sign this form or to collaborate with torture in any other way. Moreover, Dr Tzangen publicized these positions in the July 1993 issue of the IMA newsletter. Prime Minister Rabin replied swiftly to Dr Tzangen's letter, explaining that the form was being employed on an experimental basis at only one prison, and that its use would not be continued. Prime Minister Rabin's answer is questionable and evades the fundamental issue, which is the use of torture in Israeli interrogation centres.

In order to promote the struggle against torture, we cannot rely, unfortunately, on the personal ethics of citizens and physicians. We must rely on explicit regulations, on the regulations of the law. The Israeli government must pass legislation which explicitly prohibits the practice of torture in Israel.

Notes

1. The systematic practice of torture by Israeli security forces has been thoroughly documented by various international, Palestinian and Israeli organizations. Some of this work is described in the following publications:

Al-Haq (West Bank Affiliate, International Commission of Jurists), *Palestinian Victims of Torture Speak Out*, Ramallah, 1993.

Amnesty International, *Torture in the Eighties*, London, 1984. References to torture in Israel on pp. 233–6

Amnesty International, *Annual Report 1992*, London, 1992. References to torture in Israel on pp. 150–3.

Amnesty International, *Annual Report 1993*, London, 1993. References to torture in Israel on pp. 168–71.

Association of Israeli-Palestinian Physicians for Human Rights, *Activity Report July–November 1992. Focus on: Torture in Israel*, Tel Aviv, 1992.

B'Tselem, *The Interrogation of Palestinians during the Intifada: Ill-Treatment, 'Moderate Physical Pressure' or Torture?*, Jerusalem, 1991.

B'Tselem, *The Interrogation of Palestinians during the Intifada: Follow-Up to March 1991 B'Tselem Report*, Jerusalem, 1992.

Palestinian Human Rights Information Centre, *Israel's Use of Electric Shock Torture in the Interrogation of Palestinian Detainees*, Jerusalem, 1992.

Public Committee against Torture in Israel, *Moderate Physical Pressure: Interrogation Methods in Israel*, Jerusalem, 1990.

Thornhill, Teresa, *Making Women Talk*, London, Lawyers for Palestinian Human Rights, 1992.

2. Landau Commission, *Report of the Commission of Enquiry into the Methods of Investigation of the General Security Services Regarding Hostile Terrorist Activity* (the Landau Report), Jerusalem, State of Israel, 1987.

3. Amnesty International, *Israel and the Occupied Territories – Doctors and Interrogation Practices: The Case of Nader Qumsieh*, London, 1993.

4. Mr Kumsiah underwent urological treatment at Makassed Hospital in East Jerusalem after his release from prison.

5. For a detailed description and interviews with four detainees who underwent torture in Tulkarm Prison in the last month of 1992, see Avi Raz, 'Moderate physical pressure', *Ma'ariv* (Israeli daily newspaper), 4 December 1992. See also, Dorit Rishoni, 'Torture in Tulkarm', *Sharon* (Israeli weekly news magazine), 4 December 1992; and B'Tselem report, *The Death of Mustafa Barakat in the Interrogation Wing of the Tulkarm Prison*, Jerusalem, 1992.

6 The conflict between medical ethics and security measures

HERNAN REYES

Teams of physicians and delegates of the International Committee of the Red Cross (ICRC) visit prisoners all over the world.[1] In 1992 ICRC teams visited 96,300 prisoners in fifty-four countries. The aim of these visits is to try to prevent forced disappearances and any forms of torture, and to ascertain that conditions of detention are adequate. The doctors on the ICRC teams have to ascertain that health conditions in custody are adequate and that medical services are provided for all prisoners.[2] All prisoners are entitled to receive adequate medical assistance and treatment as the need arises. The level of treatment for prisoners should ideally be the same as that available for the rest of the community. Guidelines on medical services for prisoners are to be found in international, regional and national statements and recommendations.[3] A comprehensive set of guidelines for health care services in prisons was published recently in the Third General Report by the European Committee for the Prevention of Torture (1992).

In their visits worldwide, ICRC physicians are regularly confronted with situations where security considerations enter into direct conflict with the providing of health care. The word 'security' may have two different meanings in these contexts. On the one hand, the term encompasses any or all regulations for prisoners, internal or external to the prison, that relate to the enforcement of discipline and actual custody. These regulations apply to all prisoners, but may be particularly strict for certain categories of prisoners considered particularly 'dangerous'. On the other hand, security considerations in other contexts may involve actual state security forces and therefore, sometimes, certain coercive regulations or practices, particularly in the early stages of detention or interrogation. In both cases, medical ethics can and do come into conflict with security regulations, as illustrated by examples given below.

These two situations – 'enforcement of discipline' and 'state security' – have to be considered separately. In both cases, medical independence plays a paramount role in ensuring that doctors are in a position to provide adequate medical care, unconstrained by considerations that are not necessarily in the best interests of the patient.

Physicians actually working as part of police, security or armed forces personnel – and this is especially true in war or internal strife situations – are particularly vulnerable in this respect and may be subjected to such pressures. Medical doctors should be able to work in the best interests of their patients without their clinical judgement having to be overruled by non-medical criteria. This is often difficult for doctors employed by security services or armed forces. The priorities of such institutions may not necessarily coincide with a doctor's paramount interest in the health and well-being of the patient, as defined in the doctor–patient relationship essential to medical care.

In all custody situations, health care personnel, and particularly physicians, are potentially at risk of being subjected to pressure from non-medical authorities when their medical decisions conflict with the interests of management or security. For reasons that cannot be merely ignored, security personnel prefer working with physicians whom they consider to be part of the security system. 'Prison doctors' indeed may better understand the imperatives of custody personnel. Prison routine and regimes, as well as the actual working of the prison itself, may perhaps be best grasped by a physician who is fully integrated into the system, as opposed to an outside physician completely ignorant of the prison environment.

This situation certainly has its drawbacks. A physician who is too fully 'integrated' into the system may not be able to impose their views to counter security measures that may be detrimental to prisoners' health. The physician may not be in a position to appeal above the heads of their 'colleagues' so as to impose a clinical judgement when this conflicts with 'security'. Inversely, particularly in ICRC experience, prison authorities are also only too glad to have 'their own doctor', whom they know is not in a position to overrule 'imperative security considerations', often for fear of losing their position.

The dilemma of medical independence is taken a step further when physicians are actually 'incorporated' into military, police or security forces, and not just salaried by a prison administration. In this case as well, when contradictions of interest arise, physicians are caught between their loyalty to 'the service' and their own ethical obligations as physicians. Analogous situations may occur in certain cases when the 'law of the land' comes into conflict with a position taken by a doctor in accordance with medical ethics.[4]

In order to avoid the above-mentioned situations, it is extremely important that, so far as possible, prisoners receive medical attention from health care staff independent from the custodial system and the police, military or security forces involved in their arrest or safekeeping, preferably employed by a public health authority. This may often not be practical, so far as nurses or medical orderlies are concerned. However, the medical doctor ultimately responsible for medical care of prisoners should be independent of the detaining authority. Ideally, such a doctor should provide medical care for the surrounding community, and not work exclusively for the prison population. In ICRC experience, it is possible for such a physician to ensure clinical care and still have a realistic approach towards security considerations.

Examples of conflict

The following are examples of conflict between custody security and the right to medical care.

Even when prison administrations provide prisoners with adequate access to medical care, problems often arise when access to outside care is needed. The first example to consider is the case of 'enforcement of discipline'. Problems most often occur when 'high-security' prisoners are involved. Prisoners may be classified in such a category because of the nature of their offence, their escape potential or the perceived degree of danger they represent to the outside population or authority.

Several examples, taken from ICRC experience, can be given of situations where internal prison regulations come into conflict with the practice of medical care. These examples are not isolated exceptions, but rather commonly occurring situations, where doctors are sometimes hard pressed to impose their better clinical judgement.

Prisoners considered to be 'high-security' are often very difficult to transfer to outside medical establishments when they need special care or investigations. Security regulations sometimes limit these transfers to a 'one-at-a-time' basis, or only when specific custody personnel can be available. If security measures *per se* are not in question here, transfers of patients should primarily be guided by the patient's medical requirements. The physician should be able to influence decisions on such transfers according to the medical state of the prisoner in their charge.

Likewise, transportation of 'high-security' prisoners is sometimes carried out in less than optimal conditions. There have often been cases of inappropriate police or military vehicles being used for transfers of patients whose condition obviously needed a proper ambulance. Prisoners may also be handcuffed, often with their hands behind their backs, for hours on end, while waiting to receive medical attention in overheated or freezing cold vehicles, as the case may be. Once 'high-security' prisoners are actually hospitalized, their length of stay may often not be ruled by medical considerations, but may be determined by security regulations. Patients undergoing surgery, for example, who may need proper convalescence in a hospital, are sometimes rushed back to the prison for security reasons, overruling the clinical judgement of the medical staff.

Whether in the actual prison or at a referral hospital, 'high-security' prisoners are often not allowed to see the physician in private. Custody personnel are obliged by regulations to be present and within hearing distance of the doctor–patient interview. It may sometimes be true that some particularly dangerous prisoners have to remain within sight of custody personnel, so as to avoid any aggressive behaviour or possible violence towards the doctor. There should, however, be no valid reason for custody personnel to listen in on the private consultation between doctor and patient.

Another case of conflict between medical care for prisoners and security relates to actual custody during consultations. The importance of privacy for the consultation should refer not only to actual custodial staff. In most prisons, medical orderlies and even nurses are part of the prison staff. Unfortunately, their custodial role sometimes overrules their medical role, which can create conflicts of interest. Prisoners have often been known to insist on seeing the doctor on their own, as they refuse to speak in front of the staff nurse or orderly. Rightly or wrongly, prisoners often do not trust auxiliary medical personnel, whom they see as working primarily for the detaining authorities. Physicians should see to it that the confidentiality of the consultation is guaranteed, and obtain the necessary privacy within the means available. Similarly, the prisoner's medical file should be accessible only to the doctor. It should not be annexed to the prisoner's personal custody file. In specific cases where a conflict of interest between security and medical care may genuinely appear, the doctor should be able to appeal to a higher medical authority for counsel and an ultimate decision. The reason for this is that the attending 'bedside' doctor should never have to put themselves into a position where they may have to act as an auxiliary for the custodial or security services.

Custody or security personnel should also not be present during physical examinations of prisoners, in operating theatres or similar circumstances. On the physician's side, it is paramount that any doctor examining a prisoner identify themselves to the patient. This also obviously implies that no doctor should ever agree to see or examine a blindfolded or hooded patient. Communication being an essential part of any consultation, a doctor should be able to speak to the patient. They should refuse to examine any patient who, for example, is not allowed to speak to the doctor or answer questions. Doctors should never examine patients constrained by handcuffs or leg irons. Likewise, patients should not be chained or handcuffed to the examination or operating table.

A final example of security measures in prisons that may come into conflict with medical care concerns medical participation in physically enforced transfers or in applying methods of restraint. The former case can occur when a violent prisoner is to be transferred or removed forcibly from a cell. There have been cases where a physician is required to be present to ensure that minimum force is used on the prisoner. In the second case, where multiple-point handcuffing or other restraint devices are applied to a prisoner, a doctor is supposed to give approval and be responsible for the supervision of the procedure.

In both these cases it should be stressed that physicians should disassociate themselves from any such practices. If a doctor is to have any credibility with the patients entrusted to them, they cannot permit coercive practices which are violent by definition and, no matter how 'justified', cannot be said to be in the interest of the prisoner. In both these cases, there can be no substitute for adequate training of custody personnel on the use of minimum force.

Physicians as part of the repressive system

The most flagrant violations of medical ethics in conflicts between security and medical care occur when physicians actually participate in coercive or repressive measures, or even actual torture.[5] The subject of medical participation in torture has been extensively covered.[6] The World Medical Association's Declaration of Tokyo of 1975 specifically prohibits physicians from participating in any form of torture whatsoever, or using their medical knowledge to assist torturers.

Converging testimony from many sources indicates that medical participation in coercive interrogation or actual torture is widespread. There are many forms that this medical participation may take. It may involve examining prisoners prior to coercion and interrogation. It may, at the other end of the line, involve resuscitation or medical treatment of prisoners having undergone torture. It may even mean monitoring interrogation sessions. Medical participation can therefore range from mere passive condoning of torture to actual participation. More often still, numerous cases (on all continents) have been encountered of doctors who, by their silence and passive cooperation with the torturers, allow torture to persist and flourish.

The case of doctors, for example, certifying that prisoners are 'fit' for certain coercive practices, or 'fit' for interrogation (although they know that torture goes on during this phase of detention), is regularly encountered. Doctors also are called upon to 'patch up slip-ups' that occur during torture. They receive blindfolded or hooded patients from the torturers, who are not allowed to talk to them, only for specific treatment or assessment. The doctors also are not allowed to ask questions of the prisoners or may otherwise be intimidated not to. In worse scenarios still, the physicians ensure that the prisoners they see remain blindfolded, so as not to be recognized by them. This type of participation in many cases allows the repressive system to function 'smoothly'. By providing expert assessment and medical treatment, the physicians are the essential cog in the system, without which, perhaps, torture would not be possible.

Why do doctors participate in torture? Or why do some at least allow the system to go on thanks to their provision of medical care? Apart from extreme cases, where physicians participate actively in applying torture or perhaps even in devising it, the answer is often complex. Experience has shown that medical participation often comes about in an oblique way. Although there may often be some degree of coercion (fear of losing position, rank, other benefits or, in extreme cases, even their freedom or lives), many doctors convince themselves that their actions may actually be beneficial 'within the circumstances' to the victims. This is the slippery slope that doctors sometimes take, some perhaps even naively thinking that they are 'only trying to help'. Some doctors may sincerely believe that their presence can be beneficial and alleviate some of the suffering. Paradoxically, some of the victims may also be 'comforted' by the fact that a doctor is somehow involved.[7] This should not, however, cloud the essential fact that doctors should never get involved in any form of repression for any motive whatsoever. This is one issue always looked into and taken up by the physicians of the International Committee of the Red Cross when visiting prisoners and assessing medical care. The fact that doctors participate should also be a matter of extreme concern to local medical associations. Only concerted action by doctors themselves can hope to put a stop to such practices.

Conclusion

The custodial and prison environments are 'high-risk' situations for physicians, as they may be subjected to pressure from non-medical authorities who try to influence their decision-making. This is even more true when doctors work with security forces or armed personnel in situations of war or other forms of internal conflict. It is extremely important that physicians always act in the best interests of their patients, and not let themselves be influenced by non-medical rules or regulations that may contradict their better clinical judgement. Ideally, physicians working with prisoners should be independent from the security or prison staff. However, in all cases, physicians should strive not to be restrained by decisions or rules that are clearly in conflict with medical ethics. Recognized international medical guidelines, as for example those issued by the World Medical Association, should be referred to. The physicians of the International Committee of the Red Cross, in their work with prisoners worldwide, also try to do their level best to uphold medical ethics, by supporting local doctors who may be hard pressed to act on their own in the best interests of the prisoners in their charge.

Notes

1. ICRC teams visit prisoners of war in cases of international armed conflict, as well as 'security prisoners' in cases of internal strife. The issue of POWs shall not be dealt with here.

2. For a detailed description, see H. Reyes and R. Russbach, 'The role of the doctor in ICRC visits to Prisoners', *International Review of the Red Cross*, no. 284, September 1991.

3. UN Standard Minimum Rules, 1957 and 1977; National Association for the Care and Resettlement of Offenders, *Minimum Standards for Prison Establishments*, London, 1984; European Prison Rules, 1987; UN Principles of Medical Ethics (CIOMS), 1982; etc.

4. A typical case is when, for example, a judiciary authority demands that a physician force-feed a prisoner on a hunger strike.

5. There are many internationally recognized definitions of torture (e.g. World Medical Association, Tokyo, 1975; UN, Declaration on the Protection of All Persons from Being Subjected to Torture and Other Cruel, Inhuman or Degrading Treatment or Punishment, 1975 and 1984 Convention against Torture and Other Cruel, Inhuman or Degrading Treatment or Punishment). The ICRC does not have an additional one. However, it should be stressed that a whole spectrum of humiliating and degrading practices imposed on prisoners in detention should definitely be included in the subcategory officially known as 'cruel, inhuman and degrading treatment'.

6. See British Medical Association, *Medicine Betrayed: The Participation of Doctors in Human Rights Abuses*, London, Zed Books, 1992.

7. One torture victim testified, once released, that she was relieved to be taken every now and then to see a doctor, as then at least she 'knew she was not going to be killed'.

The role of codes of medical ethics
in the prevention of torture

JAMES WELSH

Medical ethics have the potential to help protect prisoners and detainees from torture by setting out, in unambiguous terms, the prohibition against medical participation in torture, and by giving doctors a clear vision of their role as guardian of the interests of their patients. Equally important, ethical codes can set out a framework of support for those doctors resisting pressure to assist in ill-treatment and can provide a standard to assess the behaviour of doctors alleged to have assisted in torture. This potential function of ethics has not been fully realized, and the purpose of this chapter is to examine the link between medical ethics and the defence of human rights, as well as to look at what measures might be needed to help medical ethics better fulfil their important protective function.

The medical profession has a long-standing body of principles governing professional behaviour. Key writings on the comportment of physicians can be traced back to antiquity; the Greek physician Hippocrates in the fifth century BC is the best known today, but in the period since the Hippocratic era important contributions have been made by Arabic, Jewish and other thinkers.[1]

The perceived relevance of medical ethics to human rights in the modern sense of the term is quite recent and was given a tragic stimulus by the outrages perpetrated by physicians during World War II. In German-occupied territories, 'eugenic' procedures and medical experiments were carried out by doctors, including highly influential members of the profession.[2] Equally horrendous, but less known, were the experiments carried out by Japanese medical researchers in Japanese-controlled territories during the same period.[3] It was as a result of these abuses that the World Medical Association (WMA) was created in 1947 with international ethical codes high on its priority list. The initial ethical statements of the WMA did not specifically address torture but, rather, set out fundamental principles with which active or passive engagement in torture was broadly incompatible. For example, the modern equivalent of the Hippocratic Oath – the Declaration of Geneva – requires the doctor to 'maintain the utmost respect for human life' and 'not [to] use ... medical knowledge contrary to the laws of humanity'. While the expression 'laws of humanity' has no juridical meaning, its general meaning would have been clear from the strong opposition felt by the international medical profession to the abuses carried out by Nazi doctors. Nevertheless, it is a rhetorical call to decency rather than a specific injunction against specific practices.

Medical involvement in abuses did not end in 1948 when the above declaration was adopted. In the following decades, European powers were drawn increasingly into protracted and vicious anti-colonial wars during which repressive measures were commonly used. Equally, in communist countries and military dictatorships, human rights violations were widely practised. Little documentation exists about the role of doctors in these abuses during the 1950s and 1960s, but it would have been very difficult for health professionals to have avoided becoming involved in the consequences of ill-treatment meted out to political prisoners during this period.

In the early 1970s the attitude of the medical profession to interrogation and ill-treatment was specifically discussed by the WMA. This resulted from proposals that the interrogation of prisoners in Northern Ireland should be carried out under medical supervision, in order to protect the prisoner from harm. The British Medical Association, which was criticized for instructing doctors not to cooperate in such interrogations, sought guidance from the WMA on the ethical role of physicians in the conflict in Northern Ireland, and specifically on the role of doctors in interrogations. The WMA undertook a review of this issue and formulated a response applicable to all member associations. The British government finally accepted a minority report of a commission of enquiry – the Parker Committee – into allegations of ill-treatment of detainees and stopped the use of the so-called 'five techniques' – hooding, wall-standing, subjection to noise, sleep deprivation, and food and drink deprivation. Had the government accepted the majority report with its recommendation of medical supervision of interrogation, 'doctors would have found themselves in the uncomfortable position of being accessories to ill-treatment sanctioned by the state; they would then have been torn between their ethical principles and their duties to a democratic society'.[4]

Also during the early to mid-1970s, allegations of the involvement of physicians in torture were being reported in Chile and other Latin American countries where military dictatorships were carrying out brutal repression. Against difficult odds, human rights organizations and victim support groups started to organize in response. During this period reports were also surfacing of the brutal misuse of psychiatry in the Soviet Union, where individuals were being compulsorily detained in psychiatric hospitals and ill-treated because of their political activities or beliefs.[5] This all added impetus to the search for forceful action on the problem of doctors and torture.

In 1975, at its Twenty-Ninth Assembly in Japan, the WMA adopted the Declaration of Tokyo, which remains the most succinct and unambiguous proscription of medical participation, or acquiescence, in torture. It is a major marker-point in the development of medical ethics and was influential in further positive developments. In the following few years, nurses', psychologists' and psychiatrists' associations added their voices against the exploitation of their professional skills for malevolent ends. In 1982, the United Nations adopted the Principles of Medical Ethics, which again prohibited medical participation or acquiescence in torture; the Principles applied to all health personnel, though they were regarded as having 'particular' relevance to physicians.

While the growing body of ethical principles are to be warmly welcomed as very positive, it is important to combat the risk that writing codes of ethics is seen as an end-product in itself, symbolizing the commitment of an association to oppose torture and other abuses. It is absolutely essential that the codes be seen as a starting point for continual monitoring, review and discipline of doctors failing to adhere to standards.

The role of doctors in torture

Doctors, and other health personnel, can be involved in acts of torture in different ways. The first, and most serious, is as an active participant in the torture (by which I mean that they inflict the torture). This appears to be rare, though hard evidence is difficult to obtain. However, two investigations by the British Medical Association,[6] and studies by Amnesty International[7] and others,[8] suggest that it is more common for the doctor to act as a medical assistant to torturers. Among the roles played by doctors in Chile during the period of military rule (1973–89) were the following: 'Evaluating the victim's capacity to withstand torture ... the provision of medical treatment if complications occur ... providing professional knowledge and skills to the torturer ... falsifying or deliberately omitting medical information when issuing health certificates or autopsy reports'.[9]

Apparently much more common is the knowledge by some doctors that colleagues are involved in torture or that they themselves are tolerating unsympathetic, negligent or cruel treatment by failing to take any action against such practices. Indeed, as one commentator suggested in a contribution to the British Medical Association's working party on medical involvement in human rights abuses: 'if these basic problems [tolerance of ill-treatment] cannot be combated, then we should not be surprised if some doctors slide into more active forms of assistance in torture'.[10]

Even in the absence of specific codes of ethics on torture, it is difficult to understand how doctors could possibly imagine medical involvement in torture to be compatible with humanitarian ethical principles. There is no simple answer, but a number of possible factors can be adduced, some of which are illustrated in the following observation made by a Chilean professor of medicine at the time of his detention in Santiago following the 1973 military coup. During his period in detention he encountered doctors working with the security forces:

> Most of the doctors were young and some had been my students. Several showed sympathy ... Others, perhaps the majority, pretended to ignore what they saw and appeared frightened to talk about it. A few justified what was happening on political grounds. One young doctor replied to me in an aggressive manner: 'What do you expect? We are at war.'[11]

It should be noted that here the doctors meeting the professor would almost certainly have known his identity and should have accorded him some respect both personally and as a result of his professional standing. Other prisoners were less likely to be accorded that respect.

For some doctors working within repressive environments, medicine has taken on a technical character, having a diminished moral dimension and directed by the ends required by their military or security colleagues. According to this view, the basic rights of the prisoner (who now ceases to be patient) are seen as practically irrelevant in this context; as one Uruguayan prison psychiatrist said with respect to the practice of systematically making clinical information available to military personnel: 'I was confined in my function. I ignored some aspects [of prison procedure] and there were some aspects I didn't want to know. It wasn't my purpose ... They were prisoners, and I was a military doctor.'[12]

Another possible factor explaining the failure of the doctor to act in the best interests of his or her patient is that medical ethics, although they are recognized by the doctor, are regarded as being in conflict with another set of overriding obligations. These usually relate to battles against crime, subversion or communism, or, more generally, to the imperative to defend national security or interests. Some doctors may feel genuine anxiety about the conflict between competing loyalties but may nevertheless, after consideration, set ethics aside. There are other doctors who, when faced with unethical demands, feel unable to resist these demands for fear of the consequences to themselves or to family members if they refuse. This latter group may well represent a large proportion of those doctors who become involved in unethical acts in the course of their work with the security forces. The problem is compounded where a doctor may be called to provide services to the security forces for a short period as a junior doctor, for example during military service. Discomfort at the role required of them can be tempered by the knowledge that they will not have to carry out this role for very long. (Paradoxically, it is the rotation of doctors in and out of such service that offers a chance for breaking the entrenchment of unacceptable practice in dealings with detainees, though, for this strategy to be effective, the incoming doctors have to have power and professional support to assert their clinical independence.[13])

Refusal to practise abusive medicine in the face of systematic coercion, while not being easy, is possible. There are some inspiring cases of doctors who refused to compromise, and whose stand was accepted by the authorities. In some cases, the resistance of the doctors meant that the abuses did not occur and established a precedent. (Of course, in other cases the authorities found other, less principled doctors or other health professionals to carry out this role.) However, it has to be recognized that such brave behaviour is aided immeasurably when the collective weight of the medical profession is behind the individual.

Statements against medical participation in torture

The two major international medical anti-torture codes, the WMA's Declaration of Tokyo and the United Nations Principles of Medical Ethics, are central to any discussion on the medical role in preventing ill-treatment. Both of these codes have been analysed in depth by the human rights lawyer Nigel Rodley, who provides an excellent analysis of their strengths and weaknesses.[14] In this chapter I will only focus on those elements relating to torture, though there are other aspects of human rights which are touched on by both standards.

The Declaration of Tokyo of the WMA states that

> The doctor shall not countenance, condone or participate in the practice of torture or other forms of cruel, inhuman or degrading procedures, whatever the offence of which the victim of such procedures is suspected, accused or guilty, and whatever the victim's beliefs or motives, and in all situations, including armed conflict and civil strife.

It is hard to read this first article of the Tokyo Declaration in any way other than as an absolute prohibition on any medical assistance in torture, including failure to report torture, though at least one commentator has suggested that the Declaration may be open to a less restrictive interpretation.[15] I will look below at the extent to which the Declaration of Tokyo is fulfilling its role as a major anti-torture code.

The second major standard applicable to the medical profession, the UN's Principles of Medical Ethics, states in principle 2 that

> It is a gross contravention of medical ethics, as well as an offence under applicable international instruments, for health personnel, particularly physicians, to engage, actively or passively, in acts which constitute participation in, complicity in, incitement to or attempts to commit torture or other cruel, inhuman or degrading treatment or punishment.

Again, this statement is, to my reading, unambiguous when read in its entirety; active or passive participation in torture is, without exception, a contravention of medical ethics. It could be argued that the drafters left a small hole in the Principles by excluding from their remit any 'pain or suffering arising only from, inherent in or incidental to, lawful sanctions to the extent consistent with the Standard Minimum Rules for the Treatment of Prisoners' (footnote 1 to the Principles), and indeed this is a significant weakness.[16] Nevertheless, the broad picture set out in the Principles is clear: no medical participation in torture.

What weak points do they have?

These two standards represent, for the one, a statement of international moral authority coming from the medical profession, and for the other, a statement with consensus agreement within the United Nations. What are their deficiencies? With regard to the Declaration of Tokyo, there are three aspects of this standard which I would like to suggest are problematic. The first is that the Declaration has uncertain status. It is a declaration – a statement of principles – and it would be difficult for member associations of the WMA to distance themselves from its message. But what about non-member associations? And can such guidance have binding force among member associations if they themselves have not formally adopted it as association policy. Are these guidelines adequately disseminated? Can a doctor be held to account for infractions against a code of which he or she is ignorant? While the answer to the last question may be 'yes', since infractions of the Declaration would also be infractions of basic medical ethics, it still begs the question as to the preventive value of a code whose existence or provisions is not widely known at grass-roots level. The question of monitoring of standards is something to which I will return below.

With regard to the Principles of Medical Ethics, some of the comments made above apply. The Principles appear not to be well known at grass-roots level and, in any event, are non-binding in a legal sense, nor subject to any evident form of disciplinary overview. There is no reporting mechanism proposed or implemented whereby infractions of the principles would be made known to appropriate bodies for their consideration and action.

Both standards do not specifically address, except in an implied or inferential way, failures of a quasi-professional nature such as inadequate medical examinations and reports. Amnesty International frequently receives allegations that doctors made cursory examinations of prisoners or wrote reports which, while perhaps not always blatantly false, nevertheless failed to adequately reflect the prisoner's allegations or physical and mental signs of ill-treatment.[17]

How are ethics put into practice?

The keys to the utility of medical ethics are the extent to which they are regarded by the practitioner, the patient, the medical association and the government as binding, and the vigour with which they are promoted and monitored. If ethics are merely advisory and optional, and moreover not well known, then there is, by definition, little force in them. I have raised above the possibility that some medical associations and individuals may see the code of ethics as being the end of a process – that of negotiating a consensus on an issue – rather than the minimum starting point from which to actively maintain and possibly change behaviour. Any lack of clarity on this issue must be dispelled.

If medical ethics are to be of any use in the fight against torture, then two things have to happen. First, the body of ethics has to be publicized, made available for reference and agreed as important by the medical profession at large and, more widely, by society. Second, infractions of ethics have to be challenged and, where necessary, disciplined. There is some evidence that protest about any kind of abuse or incompetence in a health setting is not warmly welcomed by those whose behaviour is called into question.[18] To confront an act or allegation of participation in torture requires an apparent rupture of the long-standing principle of collegiate solidarity and may require a doctor to resolve a potential conflict between their own political and ethical sympathies. The potential depth of feeling against publicizing the bad behaviour of a colleague was powerfully illustrated at the 1983 World Medical Assembly in Venice, where a proposal that doctors who torture be reported by colleagues was vigorously rejected by some of those present on the grounds that it would force doctors to become 'informers'.[19]

One practical impediment to the successful application of medical ethics to the prevention of torture is that in some countries the professional leadership is corrupt or weak and reluctant to act. In certain countries, the leadership of the medical association is closely allied to the government or the party in power or may even be appointed by the government. In such circumstances the self-disciplinary role of the professional association is certain not to function unless special circumstances dictate that they take action in a particular case. (Sometimes it is the membership which is in conflict with an ethical leadership, though in practice this has been about issues other than torture or cruel treatment.)

These difficulties all point to the need for international pressure for all national associations to agree and implement anti-torture codes, for a commitment to monitor compliance with ethical codes, and for the development of a consensus on the disciplining of doctors involved in torture. Where associations refuse to implement standards they should be forcefully asked why.

Application of codes of ethics against torture

The successful application of medical ethics to combat torture is difficult to document in a simple and direct fashion, since opposition to torture can be based on many factors – moral, political, theological, ethical – and involve different players. There are nevertheless some examples of individual and collective medical actions against human rights violations which have been important and successful initiatives. Several brief examples can be given here. The case of Northern Ireland in the early 1970s was discussed above. However, after the reforms brought in, in the wake of the Parker Committee findings, there was a resurgence in abuses coming to the attention of doctors. In 1976 and 1977 forensic medical officers, alarmed by cases of detainees showing signs of injuries sustained under police interrogation, complained successively to different levels of the police authorities before finally making their objections public after the apparent failure of a government enquiry to put a complete halt to abuses. In conjunction with press reports and an investigation by Amnesty International, the impact of these revelations was irresistible and led to changes in the conduct of police interrogations and the introduction of protective measures for prisoners.[20]

In both Chile and Uruguay, where abuses were widespread in the 1970s and early 1980s, medical associations took a number of human rights initiatives, but only after protracted periods when these associations were tightly controlled by their respective governments. In Chile, one of the first acts taken by the medical association, following its regaining in 1982 the right to conduct its own affairs, was to embark on a programme of human rights promotion, the development of a revised code of ethics and investigation into the alleged involvement of doctors in torture.[21] In Uruguay, the medical association established a national ethics convention in the last days of the military government and set up a national commission of ethics which established a rigorous protocol for the investigation of doctors alleged to have abused prisoners and detainees.[22] The association has also attempted to see legal recognition for a separation of civil function (medical care) within a military framework, and has pressed the government to grant doctors civilian status even where they work in the armed forces. (This was the situation prior to the period of military dictatorship.) In both Chile and Uruguay, those found guilty of abuses were disciplined, though it is likely that only a fraction of the doctors abusing prisoners were brought before medical tribunals and found culpable, either because many were not identified, or because the evidence against those accused was inadequate.

The Turkish Medical Association (TMA), like the Chilean and Uruguayan medical associations, was effectively put out of action following a military coup, in this case in 1980. Following the lifting of the suspension of the association at the end of 1983, it was seriously constrained in what it was permitted to do within the law. However, it started a programme of human rights promotion and investigated the numerous allegations of medical assistance in torture, including the writing of false medical certificates. Like the Uruguayan association, the TMA has seen the status of doctors working with the military change from being purely medical to being 'first and foremost soldiers'.[23] It is working to reverse this militarization of medicine. The TMA has also undertaken investigations into specific cases of deaths in custody and publicized their findings and criticisms, besides examining human rights abuses and the position of doctors in the south-east of the country. (In the south-east there is a significant level of abuses and large-scale military activity, together with armed opposition by Kurdish activists seeking autonomy or independence for the Kurdish people.)[24]

There have also been many failures of medical ethics to protect prisoners or to bring pressure for reforms after abuses have occurred. For example, the Medical Association of South Africa (MASA) failed to act properly in response to the behaviour of the doctors treating the Black Consciousness activist Steve Biko, who died in 1977 following assault by prison officers. The doctors clearly failed to adequately care for their patient, but first the South African Medical and Dental Council and subsequently MASA found them to have behaved without fault.[25] In general, the association failed to address the issues of torture and the role of doctors in protecting their prisoner-patients, a failure which drew criticism both internationally and also from doctors within South Africa, some of whom established an anti-apartheid professional association. Even where the medical profession intervened to assert what it thought was a positive role, it laid itself open to criticism. Thus, the code of principles for the treatment of children in detention was criticized for not containing an explicit condemnation of the detention of children for political reasons. The South African Paediatric Association, which had drafted the code of principles in 1987, subsequently made clear its opposition to the detention of children without trial and to the abuse of children.[26]

During the 1980s, in South Africa, emergency regulations were in place, and the medical profession was overwhelmingly dominated by politically conservative doctors who were unrepresentative of the majority of the population, particularly of those who were the victims of human rights violations.[27] Nevertheless, even within this negative framework, the courageous actions of a number of doctors deserve mention. Dr Wendy Orr took action in the South African court system to protect the emergency detainees she was seeing who showed signs of injuries sustained at the hands of the security forces.[28] The pathologist Dr Jonathan Gluckman eventually resorted to the press when his evidence of persistent and lethal violence inflicted on detainees was not taken seriously by the authorities. His findings were influential in forcing the issue of ill-treatment and deaths of detainees back on to the national political agenda.

Towards the end of the 1980s, MASA started to make statements and adopt resolutions reflecting an important change in its position on human rights. For example, in June 1989 the MASA Federal Council belatedly 'share[d] the concerns of other organizations about the health hazards of detention without trial' and went on to deplore the practice. Subsequently, with a continuing process of reform within MASA, there was a *rapprochement* with the anti-apartheid National Medical and Dental Association. MASA eventually published what amounted to an apology for its failings in the Biko case.

What is needed?

There is an immediate need for wider dissemination of basic ethical texts, as well as a more profound discussion of the link between medical ethics and the prevention of torture. There is some evidence to suggest that ethical statements on torture are not widely known at grass-roots level. While these codes may not be perfect, they are more than adequate to establish basic standards of behaviour and should be promoted among medical students and qualified medical personnel. Moreover, medical associations which have not already done so should make clear that they support international codes prohibiting medical involvement in torture or other human rights violations.

In addition, there remains a need to review current ethics. This is not an innovative idea. All medical ethics standards should be kept under periodic review, since regular review helps to determine whether the standard meets the current need. Of particular importance are the following points, which are not adequately dealt with in current standards.

There needs to be more discussion about ways to more actively support doctors who wish to act in conformity with medical ethics but who are under pressure to collaborate actively or passively in state-sponsored repression. It is leaving individual doctors with extremely difficult choices if the decision to stand up to military or security force must be taken entirely by them as individuals. The nearest that either of the two major codes comes to addressing this issue is paragraph 6 in the WMA's Declaration of Tokyo, which promises, in a rather unspecific way, the support of the WMA to any doctor resisting pressure to commit abuses. The question is: What support can or will be given? How and in what circumstances? The WMA has written to governments about detained doctors, and its Secretary General visited Chile in 1986 in support of the leaders of the Chilean Medical Association who had been arrested and imprisoned. While admirable, however, this does not constitute a systematic programme, and more thought has to be given to this important role.

The Chilean Medical Association appears to have tried to recognize its role in supporting doctors by requiring, through their code of ethics, that any doctor pressured to commit an unethical act should report the fact to the association. Since the association has had a record of taking up ethical issues with the government, this procedure has both logic and credibility as an anti-torture measure, though little information is available about the working of this scheme in practice.

The subject of human rights and ethics cannot be left solely to the organized medical profession, however. A vital role can, and must, be played by human rights bodies, including those with a medical focus, in bringing individual cases and human rights issues to the attention of governments, medical associations and the public. The 1993 conference organized by the Association of Israeli-Palestinian Physicians for Human Rights and the Public Committee against Torture in Israel[29] is a good example of an important subject being raised publicly for open discussion and action. Following concern expressed at this meeting about the use of 'fitness for interrogation' forms on which doctors certified prisoners as fit for various forms of possible ill-treatment, the Israeli Medical Association instructed its members not to use such forms, since to do so would be incompatible with the Declaration of Tokyo.[30]

A final point for the future – what can be done to deal more effectively at national and international level with infractions of medical ethics? What should be done about associations which harbour wrong-doers, or fail to assert the primacy of medical ethics? How can the major medical organizations be brought into the process more actively? Up until now, the performance of international bodies has not been encouraging.[31] The case of South Africa was cited above; equally, the silence of medical bodies in other countries about abuses in their territory, some involving doctors (or having doctors as victims), is disturbing. Nevertheless, as illustrated above, some medical associations have made important advances in addressing these difficult questions. What is lacking is an international lead. The World Health Organization sees itself as playing a very passive role on this subject; the major international medical bodies have yet to develop an effective strategy for action to address the problem of medical involvement in torture, even though, to their credit, they have made very clear their moral and ethical opposition to the practice. Where the individual national association is not dealing effectively with the problem of medical involvement in torture, it is important that a strong international voice is heard.

Conclusion

In spite of well-documented failings, medical ethics offer both a set of guidelines for relationships between doctors and their imprisoned patients, and an analytical tool for assessing the behaviour of doctors choosing, or required, to work with prisoners or detainees. Such ethics should be promoted to prevent the betrayal of medical skills embodied by the doctor's participation in torture. And those doctors at risk of coercion to carry out unethical acts need the support of colleagues and professional associations. The latter should give a very clear message to governments that doctors will not tolerate the abuse of medical skills for political ends. If medical associations do not take the lead in this, they are failing those doctors who are forced to bear alone the heavy burden of defending basic human rights.

Notes

1. The development of medical ethics in the ancient world is discussed in A. Castoglioni, *A History of Medicine*, 2nd edn, New York, Knopf, 1947.
2. R.J. Lifton, *The Nazi Doctors: Medical Killing and the Psychology of Geno-*

cide, London, Papermac, 1986. It should be noted that so-called eugenic medical programmes had been undertaken in both North America and Europe in the early years of the century without attracting major criticism.

3. P. Williams and D. Wallace, *Unit 731*, London, Grafton, 1990.

4. M. Phillips and J. Dawson, *Doctors' Dilemmas: Medical Ethics and Contemporary Science*, Brighton, Harvester Wheatsheaf, 1985, p. 105. As Phillips and Dawson go on to say, doctors subsequently found themselves in precisely this position later in the 1970s when ill-treatment of prisoners recommenced in Northern Ireland. That these abuses were exposed was due in large measure to the reports emanating from doctors examining injured detainees.

5. S. Bloch and P. Reddaway, *Russia's Political Hospitals*, London, Gollancz, 1977.

6. See British Medical Association, *The Torture Report*, London, 1986, and *Medicine Betrayed: The Participation of Doctors in Human Rights Abuses*, London, Zed Books, 1992.

7. Amnesty International, *Involvement of Medical Personnel in Abuses against Detainees and Prisoners* (AI Index: ACT 75/08/90), London, 1990, and *Doctors and Torture*, London, Bellew, 1991.

8. H.D. Petersen and O.V. Rasmussen, 'Medical appraisal of allegations of torture and the involvement of doctors in torture', *Forensic Science International*, no. 53, 1992, pp. 97–116.

9. Chilean Medical Association report, 'The participation of physicians in torture', 1986, in E. Stover, *The Open Secret: Torture and the Medical Profession in Chile*, Washington, DC, American Association for the Advancement of Science (AAAS), 1987, p. 75.

10. H. Bamber (Director, Medical Foundation for the Care of Victims of Torture, London), letter to BMA, cited in BMA, *Medicine Betrayed*, op. cit., p. 61.

11. A. Jadresic, 'Doctors and torture: an experience as a prisoner', *Journal of Medical Ethics*, no. 6, 1980, pp. 124–8.

12. M.G. Bloche, *Uruguay's Military Physicians: Cogs in a System of State Terror*, Washington, DC, AAAS, 1987, p. 16.

13. Rotation of prison medical staff was a recommendation of the BMA working party on medical involvement in human rights violations which published its report in 1992. See recommendations 17 and 18 in *Medicine Betrayed*, op. cit., p. 198.

14. See N. Rodley, *The Treatment of Prisoners under International Law*, Oxford, Clarendon Press, 1987, chapter 12, 'Codes of professional ethics'.

15. Bloche, for example, suggests that 'the language [of the Declaration of Tokyo] does not clearly address physicians who perform their routine technical task of diagnosis and treatment without regard for its context, where that context is an organized program of torture administered by others but modulated by the physician's work product': Bloche, *Uruguay's Military Physicians*, op. cit., p. 36. I read the Declaration as more strongly opposed to such a 'technical' role inasmuch as it prohibits 'condoning' torture, which in my view includes taking no action when confronted by knowledge of torture. However, the fact that this

code is, and more generally most ethical codes are, open to interpretation emphasizes the need both for care in drafting and for the development of a body of 'case law' in the interpretation of the code.

16. The Standard Minimum Rules are not a strong protection for prisoners, and this exclusion clause opens up an area of ambiguity with respect to the infliction of cruel punishments having the character of torture. See Rodley, *The Treatment of Prisoners* ..., op. cit.

17. For consideration of this issue, see Amnesty International. *Involvement of Medical Personnel in Abuses* ..., op. cit.; BMA, *Medicine Betrayed*, op.cit. A specific case is that of Nader Qumsieh (Kumsiah), who says his complaints of torture were not recorded in medical certificates and whose scrotal injury was attributed by a doctor to the prisoner's falling downstairs; see Amnesty International, *Israel and the Occupied Territories – Doctors and Interrogation Practices: The Case of Nader Qumsieh* (AI Index: MDE 15/09/93), London, 1993.

18. K.J. Lennane, '"Whistle-blowing": a health issue', *British Medical Journal*, no. 307, 1993, pp. 667–70.

19. Rodley, *The Treatment of Prisoners* ..., op. cit., p. 299.

20. See Amnesty International, *Torture in the Eighties*, London, 1984, pp. 57–60.

21. See Amnesty International, *Human Rights in Chile: The Role of the Medical Profession* (AI Index: AMR 22/36/86), London, 1986; E. Stover, *The Open Secret: Torture and the Medical Profession in Chile*, Washington, DC, AAAS, 1986; F. Rivas, *Traición a Hipocrates*, Santiago, CESEM, 1990. In the period before and after the 1973 military coup, the medical association was split between those supporting military intervention and strong measures and those supporting the constitutional government. As the repression continued and deepened, the association, while still reflecting different political tendencies, developed a strong consensus against abuses. See Stover, *The Open Secret*, op. cit.

22. See G. Martirena, *La tortura y los médicos*, Montevideo, Ed. de la Banda Ora, 1988.

23. According to the Executive Director of the Turkish Medical Association, Dr Ugur Cilasun, military doctors before the coup studied in civilian hospitals and therefore took a civilian outlook into their practice. They were, moreover, obliged to register with the TMA. After the establishment of the military medical school, 'military doctors were expected and obliged to give priority to the chain-of-command, above and over the medical code of ethics. Shortly afterwards, medical doctors were forbidden to become registered members of the TMA': U. Cilasun, 'Torture and the participation of doctors', *Journal of Medical Ethics*, no. 17 (supplement), 1991, pp.21–2.

24. Amnesty International, *Turkey: Human Rights and the Medical Profession in the Southeast* (AI Index: EUR 44/17/93), London, 1993.

25. M. Rayner, *Turning a Blind Eye? Medical Accountability and the Prevention of Torture in South Africa*, Washington, DC, AAAS, 1987; D. Silove, 'Doctors and the state: lessons from the Biko case', *Social Science and Medicine*, no. 30, 1990, pp. 417–29. Two doctors were later found guilty of improper behaviour and disciplined. One of them later admitted his failures and apologized in a

press article ('An apology on Biko', *New York Times*, 24 October 1991).

26. AAAS, *Apartheid Medicine: Health and Human Rights in South Africa*, report based on an AAAS mission of enquiry to South Africa in April 1989, Washington, DC, 1990, p. 88.

27. According to figures cited in the 1990 AAAS report, only 5 per cent of qualified doctors in South Africa were non-white (though the source for this figure was undated and it may refer to the situation around 1980). Entry figures in English-speaking medical schools at the end of the 1980s showed a much higher entry level of non-white students; at Afrikaner schools the numbers tended to be lower than in the English-speaking schools: *Apartheid Medicine*, op. cit., pp. 38–9.

28. M. Rayner, *Turning a Blind Eye?*, op. cit., pp. 67–79.

29. Conference on The International Struggle against Torture and the Case of Israel, 13–14 June 1993, Tel Aviv, Israel.

30. J. Siegel-Itzhovich, 'Israeli doctors banned from role in interrogation', *British Medical Journal*, no. 307, 1993, p. 152.

31. For a critical review of the WMA, see T., Richards,. 'The World Medical Association: can hope triumph over experience?', *British Medical Journal*, no. 308, 1994, pp. 262–6.

8 Where is the Israeli Medical Association?

MAMDOUH AL-AKER

In 1983 a Palestinian human rights organization, Al-Haq, wrote to the Israeli Medical Association (IMA), asking for its assistance in performing an investigation. Former Palestinian prisoners alleged that doctors and other medical personnel had been involved in their torture while under interrogation. The result of Al-Haq's plea for assistance was a hasty press release issued by the IMA in which they denounced the human rights organization.

In 1983 it was possible for Israeli medical professionals not only to repudiate the notion of a connection with the torture and maltreatment of Palestinian prisoners, but to attempt to dismiss the existence of such practices totally. Today this is more difficult. The steadily growing stacks of reports and statements from Israeli and Palestinian organizations, Amnesty International and the Red Cross cannot be denied. Attempts to do so include the disingenuous methods of Rabbi Shlomo Goren, who dismissed B'Tselem's important report concerning torture[1] on the grounds that the authors were traitors and thus not made 'in the image of God'.

And yet the IMA maintains its silence. As a physician, I do not think my colleagues in Israel are convinced by inhumane reasoning such as that of Rabbi Goren. Therefore I ask, as a genuine and heartfelt enquiry, where is the Israeli Medical Association? After the Landau Commission, after the B'Tselem report, after the daily newspapers, this is a highly relevant question. While I do not claim a unique angelic status for my profession, our code of ethics and our professional life are devoted to the health and integrity of the human body. Torture, as a profound violation of the body and spirit, must therefore arouse our deepest opposition. Because I think that Israeli medical professionals sincerely believe in this code, I ask my question with sincere puzzlement and disquiet. I warmly acknowledge and have wholeheartedly participated in the efforts of the Association of Israeli-Palestinian Physicians for Human Rights to break this deadly silence, though I am aware that our efforts do not reach the majority of Israeli medical practitioners.

My question is particularly relevant because of the fact that these doctors, and the IMA which speaks for them, are not merely spectators in the terrible drama which transpires between the interrogator and his victim. The interpenetration of Israeli medical professionals and the military is a striking feature where reserve duty is regular and doctors frequently employ their skills in army uniform. For torture, especially the systematic, routine and pervasive torture and maltreatment practised against Palestinian prisoners while under interrogation, implicates many people who may stand outside the shadowy realm of the General Security Services (GSS) and the interrogation cells, but nonetheless are part of the system that maintains these cells. Doctors spend their military service practising their professions in a military setting and lend legitimacy to the practice of torture through their passive silence when in contact with a Palestinian detainee who has suffered torture.

My convictions concerning the issue of torture in Israel and the Occupied Territories are related to my personal experience with the Israeli detention system.

On the morning of 27 February 1991, I was summoned to appear at the Israeli military headquarters in Ramallah. I was told neither the reasons for the summons nor the length of time the matter would take. An operation I was supposed to have performed that morning had to be rescheduled for the afternoon.

I was made to wait all morning in the military headquarters, and conversation with officials in the afternoon concerned merely the general political situation. I was refused permission to perform the operation, and only after lengthy argument was I allowed to phone the hospital to cancel it. I was forbidden to inform them of my situation. In the evening I was presented with a document in Hebrew (a language I do not understand) that they claimed to be an arrest warrant. Requests to speak with my lawyer or a delegate from the Red Cross were refused, and my enquiries as to the nature of the charges against me were ignored. They claimed they could detain me and deny access to a lawyer for up to 180 days.

My concern for my patients, several of whom required immediate attention for life-threatening conditions, was ignored. 'Forget about them and worry about yourself,' I was told. I therefore decided to go on hunger-strike until I was allowed to attend to my patients. This lasted four days, ending on the fifth day of my detention, at which time I was allowed to write instructions for the treatment of my patients.

While in detention I was subject to objectionable conditions. The clothes I was given were dirty and smelled of urine; I was held in a cell measuring approximately 180 cm by 150 cm, with a hole in the floor for a toilet which was very smelly and dirty; the light in the cell was on at all times; occasionally I was woken in the middle of the night and moved to another cell; I was frequently hooded, often led with my hands cuffed behind my back, dragged by the edge of the hood; I was forced to withstand periods in which I was denied access to a toilet. I was kept in solitary confinement for the first thirty-five days of detention.

I was deprived of sleep for sixty hours before my first court appearance. In court I was forbidden from speaking with anyone, including my wife. My lawyer's petition for release on bail was refused, and my detention was extended. After appearing in court I was allowed to see a delegate from the Red Cross, who provided me with underwear sent by my family – my first opportunity to change my underwear since my arrest fifteen days earlier.

Following my lawyer's appeal to the Israeli High Court of Justice, I was first allowed to meet with him alone on the twenty-seventh day of detention. My case had attracted public attention, which I believe to have affected the conditions in which I was kept. The little which I was able to see and hear around me in the jail (primarily screams in the night) indicated that others were worse off than myself.

On the thirty-first day, I learned that the authorities were applying for a further extension of my detention. I decided to take a vow of silence and refuse to cooperate with my interrogators in any way. This angered them, and after four days of silence my interrogation came to an end. On the thirty-fifth day of my detention I was transferred to a prison cell with eight other detainees until the next court session, which was on 7 April.

It was never entirely clear what I was to be charged with. They made accusations that I had written leaflets for the Intifada, which is untrue. I was explicit about my political views, which I had already made abundantly clear in articles written in the Israeli press and at seminars in which I had participated. Throughout the period of detention, I was pressured to make a false, self-incriminating confession, which I refused to do.

On 7 April, the judge gave the prosecution ten more days with which to prepare charges, during which time I was to be released on bail. Forty days of detention had come to an end.

No charges have ever been made against me.

While I did not suffer torture in its most brutal forms, the treatment which I was subject to is clearly unacceptable, and is in fact torture. Not only was my detention an unjustified violation of my own personal freedom, it also compromised my ability to fulfil my professional obligations as a physician to such a degree that the well-being of my patients was jeopardized. At the time of my detention one of my patients was practically lying on the operating table waiting for my attention. Further operations and examinations of patients in life-threatening situations were scheduled for the following days. I was the doctor most familiar with their conditions, and therefore best able to treat them.

Is this of no concern to the IMA? Can it be true that this esteemed organization of Israeli physicians has so little regard for a Palestinian colleague?

Furthermore, can the IMA be totally unconcerned with the role its members are playing in the torture of detainees in Israeli detention facilities? As a signatory of the World Medical Association's Declaration of Tokyo, the IMA is obligated to insure that its members in no manner comply with the torture of detainees. Other cases, much worse than my own, can be cited as grounds for criticism of the role which Israeli health professionals play in the practice of torture.

Upon arrival at Hebron Central Prison in February 1992, Birzeit University student Amin Amin informed the prison doctor examining him of the chronic liver disease with which he was afflicted, and that he was under medical supervision. He also told his interrogators, who used the information to mock him. His interrogation included confinement in a closet and occasional beatings and blows, particularly to his stomach, which continued even after he started vomiting.[2]

A medic, and later the prison doctor, instructed Amin to take Maalox, despite his protests that he had been treated with a stronger medicine. The medic brought him Maalox three times a day. All the while the interrogation continued, including position abuse (being tied to a pipe), sleeplessness and confinement in near-freezing conditions. On the fourth day, after prolonged vomiting, he was transferred to Hadassah, where a Dr Zamir examined him, issued a medical certificate and returned him to Hebron Prison, where he was placed in an unventilated cell. In the morning the prison doctor gave him a pill. During a hearing in Hebron Military Court concerning an extension of detention, Amin began vomiting and was returned to his cell. The judge extended detention while ordering Amin be hospitalized within ninety-six hours. Instead, he was released without charge the next day, a senior officer telling him: 'Get out of here. Die at home, not here.'

It is bizarre to imagine an interrogation that included periodic breaks for the prisoner to take Maalox, and it was a parody of medical treatment for a doctor and a medic dutifully to present such an improper palliative to a very sick young man. The doctor also recommended that

Amin be moved to a warmer cell, apparently resulting in a move to a slightly 'warmer' closet, where, by Amin's estimate, temperatures hovered around five degrees Celsius.

One wonders if this might have been the same doctor and medic who earlier had failed to treat Mustafa Akawi. Mr Akawi had died in the same interrogation section of Hebron Central Prison a few weeks earlier, on 4 February 1992, of a heart attack induced by his extended exposure to freezing temperatures and other forms of torture and maltreatment. In Mr Akawi's case, after twelve days of interrogation in which he was subject to hooding, beating, position abuse and exposure to cold, a judge, while ordering an eight-day extension of detention, also ordered a medical examination. Instead, Mr Akawi was returned to prison and examined in the evening by the paramedic. At 3:30 a.m., after Mr Akawi complained of severe chest pains and shortness of breath, the Israeli interrogator contacted the medic, who failed to recognize the signs of a heart attack, later recognized by the doctor called thirty minutes after, following Mr Akawi's collapse. No ambulance was called, and Mustafa Akawi was pronounced dead at 5:20 a.m.

Here there is no doubt that the medical care was tragically inadequate, but, for the purposes of my enquiry, what is paramount is the acquiescence to the authority of the interrogator. The failure of human concern and the cursory medical attention stem, one feels, not simply from inadequate training or stretched resources, but from a failure of perception, a failure to acknowledge the deadly dangers to the health and well-being of any Palestinian detainee in the hands of GSS interrogators.

The fact that Amin Amin met these same conditions only a few weeks later, including the extended exposure to cold, is more than physically chilling.

Mustafa Barakat, 23, died of an acute attack of bronchial asthma in the GSS interrogation wing of Tulkarem Prison on 4 August 1992. He had been examined by a prison medic upon admission to the prison, after which he was allowed to keep his inhaler, and was examined again after an asthma attack during interrogation on 3 August. It is likely that the attack was triggered by interrogation practices, which included prolonged hooding. On the morning of 4 August, a physician, Dr Eli Waldner, examined him and noticed that he had 'diffused wheezing in both lungs'. He ordered an additional inhaler but did not order that the interrogation be halted, although a military source told B'Tselem that it was later decided not to hood Mustafa. The next time Dr Waldner was to see Mustafa Barakat, he was dead or dying.

I have reflected on Dr Waldner's act – a gesture of standard medical care made in total disregard, or perhaps disavowal, of the context in which the care was extended. Dr Waldner, like other prison doctors and all Israeli Defence Force personnel, is not allowed to enter the interrogation wing, which is under the strict control of the GSS. Yet he obviously has knowledge of GSS practices and might have been the one to recommend that Mustafa Barakat no longer be subjected to hooding. In this case, he returned a young man with obvious signs of physical distress to interrogation with nothing more than an additional inhaler. Can it be not only that the GSS wing is closed to him physically, but that he has also shut it out psychologically? Can it be that Israeli doctors – and Israeli society itself – have performed the same comforting mental operation?

It is time to reverse this closure, and let the light of common humanity fall inside the long-forbidden arena, seen only by the interrogators and the thousands of Palestinians who have entered its various portals. Despite a painful legacy of silence, I believe Israeli medical professionals can have a role in the opening of these doors to public scrutiny and accountability. They can demand that medical staff have immediate and open access to detainees, even under interrogation. They can support legislation and regulations that enforce standard medical ethics. They can encourage the reporting of all incidents of the maltreatment of detainees. They can better inform prison medical staff about their responsibilities concerning the well-being of prisoners, as well as the doctors and medical staff in the Israeli hospitals which often treat Palestinian detainees. Israeli medical professionals have the opportunity to initiate an honest dialogue with their Palestinian counterparts to explore the reality of abuse and the remedies to it.

The IMA has the clear obligation to speak out on all of the matters which I have mentioned above, as well as making a clear and forthright condemnation of torture and maltreatment in all its forms. The IMA must provide explicit guidelines which clarify the responsibilities of its members to guarantee the well-being of those detained by the Israeli security forces. Unfortunately, the only interruption of the IMA's silence throughout these long years of suffering in Israeli detention centres has been the occasional justification and approval of existing practices. In September 1989, Dr Ram Yishai, then IMA President, in a report to the World Medical Association, asserted among other things that 'What is called the dispersal of demonstrations is nothing but a state of war.' How can one continue defending the acts of the Israeli security forces after it has been made evident that torture is practised systematically in Israeli prisons? How can one continue justifying the acts of the Israeli security forces in the wake of Defence Minister Rabin's 'breaking bones' policy? It is this kind of mentality – the need to defend and justify every act of the Israeli security forces – that urgently needs to be addressed if the system that encourages and sustains torture is ever to be dismantled.

This need to justify and defend led to the secret portion of the Landau Commission Report and the commission's official approval of torture and maltreatment in its condoning the use of 'moderate physical pressure'. The light that needs to fall on GSS cells must also fall on the portion of the Landau Report which is kept from the public eye. This secret text, pertaining to permissible forms of physical and psychological pressure, must be one of the only official sanctions of torture and maltreatment in a democratic and open society. This sanction urgently needs to be exposed and annulled, and a total ban on torture and maltreatment declared and enforced.

On 30 April 1992, the Palestinian delegation in Washington presented a brief argument to the Israeli negotiating team calling for a halt to the torture and maltreatment of Palestinian detainees. This request was never answered. I believe it is time for those not in government – yet nonetheless implicated in its actions – to speak out. I sincerely hope that Israeli physicians and medical personnel will be among the first and most effective.

Notes

1. B'Tselem, *The Interrogation of Palestinians during the Intifada: Ill-Treatment, 'Moderate Physical Pressure' or Torture?*, Jerusalem, 1991.

2. The information concerning this and the following cases is derived from interviews conducted by B'Tselem and published in their report, *The Interrogation of Palestinians during the Intifada: Follow-Up to March 1991 B'Tselem Report*, Jerusalem, 1992.

Workshop: codes of medical ethics as a tool in the struggle against torture

led by JAMES WELSH

The subject of this workshop was the application of professional codes of ethics in the service of human rights. A given profession's code of ethics serves as a guideline for its members' conduct. This becomes relevant to an issue such as torture for members of those professions, such as medics, nurses and physicians, who might come into contact with the practice of torture while fulfilling professional duties.

Codes of ethics are to be evaluated by two criteria in order to determine their efficacy as instruments for the protection of human rights: their content and their operability, the latter concerning how well they can be implemented in the field and fulfil the expressed intention.

Codes of ethics as an instrument for the prevention of torture must strike a balance between generality and specificity. If codes are rhetorical and general statements of moral principle which lack precision, they may attract little opposition but are of limited usefulness. On the other hand, if statements very precisely define those practices prohibited they may be more controversial and may be interpreted as permitting practices not specifically proscribed. The current international ethical standards applicable to torture appear to have struck an adequate balance, though there remain some weaknesses in their application, as discussed below.

Once formulated, there are often difficulties in the enforcement of a code of ethics. How is discipline to be enforced on colleagues, particularly in a profession as conservative as the medical profession, in which collegial solidarity is such a prized principle? Positive reforms in this area can be initiated by medical association leaders or from among the membership. Leadership can sometimes be slow to react to the need for reform and can sometimes impede moves coming from within the membership. In other cases, the leadership cannot, or will not, move on reforms because of its perception of resistance to change among the membership.

In the case of Israel, the Israeli Medical Association has endorsed the Declaration of Tokyo, which is the standard document underlying medical codes of ethics concerning torture. A shortcoming in the Declaration of Tokyo is the lack of an explicit provision which obliges a physician to report acts of torture committed by others, for example in prisons where a doctor might actually witness the practice of torture or treat a detainee suffering from injuries resulting from torture. Except in those instances where there is actually a physican participating in the act of torture, the Israeli Medical Association does not demand of its members that they report incidents of torture of which they have become aware.

There is a problem of dual allegiance in the case of Israeli physicians working in the detention system. In effect, prison doctors serve two clients: the prison system and the prisoners themselves. The nature of this problem compromises the quality of care offered by the doctor to their patient, the prisoner, as decisions are influenced by non-medical considerations such as security concerns.

Proposals for action

The workshop produced several suggestions towards articulating codes of ethics and mobilizing medical associations in such a manner as to encourage physicians to assist in the struggle against torture.

1 Efforts should be made to better educate physicians employed in the detention system regarding the paramount nature of their obligation to their patient, the prisoner, and make them aware of the practical consequences of this relationship. Prison doctors must be made aware of their obligation (and right) to refuse to carry out the demands of the security services where these conflict with the medical needs and the basic human rights of the prisoner. Further, doctors must be made aware of their obligation to report any acts of torture of which they are aware, either as direct witnesses or through their treatment of detainees suffering from injuries which represent evidence of the practice of torture.

    To this end, human rights organizations can work to articulate guidelines to be given to physicians employed in the detention system. Workshops designed to better educate prison physicians about human rights could also be arranged by such organizations.

2 Human rights organizations should make an effort to encourage medical schools to better educate their students concerning questions regarding human rights in general, and complicity in torture in particular.

3 A 'hot-line' allowing physicians employed in the detention system to

anonymously report cases of torture which they may witness or suspect would facilitate them in fulfilling this responsibility while minimizing their personal risk, which might otherwise inhibit them from doing so. As a matter of principle, the Israeli Medical Association would be the appropriate body to undertake such a function, though an independent human rights body may be able to play such a role with greater perceived independence.

4 Directives ought to be given to prison staff that reports of ill-treatment will be taken very seriously; those found culpable after investigation will be punished.

5 The video-recording of interrogations might assist the prevention of acts of torture. In this event, steps would be required so as to install safeguards against the editing of such films and the 'softening up' of suspects before the video camera is turned on.

6 Steps should be taken to encourage the IMA to do what is necessary to ensure that medical reports and autopsy reports be delivered in timely order when requested by Palestinian patients or their families, particularly in cases concerning prisoners.

Note

The workshop was attended by Israeli physicians and psychologists, members of various Israeli and Palestinian human rights organizations and representatives from human rights organizations from abroad.

PART III

The legal struggle against torture

9 The history of the legal struggle against torture in Israel

FELICIA LANGER

The first complaint concerning the torture of a Palestinian came to my attention at the beginning of 1968. The complaint was passed on to me by the parents of my client, after they had received their son's blood-covered shirt. After a number of days I was finally able to visit him in Hebron Prison; however, he was too frightened to provide me with any details.

I received further complaints in March 1968 from detainees living in East Jerusalem. They told of threats and humiliations, of being hung from hooks and of severe beatings. In addition to the complaints which I sent to the authorities, I worked to move the issue forward by conducting 'mini-trials' against accepting confessions extracted under interrogation as valid testimony.[1] My argument was that they were obtained illegally through the use of force.

Already at that time one could detect two important purposes behind the use of torture. The first was the extraction of a confession through the yielding of information by the detainee concerning him or herself and others. The second purpose was an attempt to humiliate and crush the detainee.

The courts were characterized by an utter lack of faith in the testimonies of those claiming to have been tortured, while sympathy was granted openly to the police and to the Shabak (General Security Services). In that early period of the Occupation, the very existence of the Shabak was denied by the Israeli authorities, and the official response to such claims were accredited to the wild imaginations of prisoners. One of the former Shabak interrogators whose abuses produced many complaints from prisoners was an individual whose code name was Abu-Hani. His existence was denied by the Military Prosecutor. Co-incidentally, I came to discover this Abu-Hani when another person called out his name while I was standing nearby. The prosecutor was thus forced to summon Abu-Hani to court in order to respond to the complaints of the accused. His testimony from the witness stand was characterized by disrespect, insolence and cynicism. I was later to learn that I had then encountered one of the archetypes of Shabak interrogators, and that the court would not doubt anything that came out of their mouths for years as they continued their activities.

From the responses I received from hundreds of complaints which I had sent over the years, I was to learn about the symbiotic relationship which exists between the Shabak and the police, which also includes the judicial and medical personnel.

During the early 1970s, there were prisoners who became insane, such as Omar Salamah. Others suffered the impairment of bodily functions, such as Nader Afuri. Some, such as Ziad El Azaa, suffered neurological damage due to electrical shocks, and there were some left physically handicapped, like Muhammad Katmash.

In the same period of time, we began to receive complaints about the torture of Druze prisoners from Ramat Hagolan. We conducted mini-trials concerning their confessions in Kuneitra and in Majdal Shams. Later, in 1974, we conducted mini-trials involving detainees from the Palestinian National Front. My meetings with them following their appeals to the Supreme Court were like a nightmare. Descriptions of torture at the hands of the Shabak were verified by the marks on their bodies, which were still fresh. These injuries included knees damaged by forced crawling, feet swollen from blows, skin burned by chemical materials, backs bent by intense blows to the back of the neck, and wrists and hands damaged by hanging. I encountered people who had been subject to starvation, chaining, deprivation of sleep and blows to the entire body, particularly the genitals. While visiting Sulaiman Najab, I was prevented by a man from the Shabak from seeing his leg, which had been injured by torture. The Shabak officer was an intelligent man, a lover of Arab poetry, about which he used to talk with Sulaiman. He never hurt Sulaiman because this was not his job.

Official investigation of our complaints, which was ordered by the Supreme Court in an injunction following the plea which I submitted on the issue, was characterized by the concealing of evidence and by false testimonies delivered by members of the Shabak. In one case, a Shabak officer denied having ever seen the wounds of the complainant, despite the fact that we saw them together in Jalame Prison. The judges rejected the injunction, stating that the investigation had been properly conducted, and that the plaintiffs did not succeed in proving the validity of their complaint.

The Supreme Court's decision provided the Shabak with significant support. Given the opportunity to escape without punishment in such a clear case, the Shabak understood that it was possible to maintain the same procedures. Shabak personnel continued their practice of torture, aided by the silent complicity of the press, despite the complaints and protests of a minority among the Israeli public.

Up until 1984, we continued to deliver complaints to the military courts, which continued to display full faith in the denials of the Shabak personnel. There was only one brief period, which cannot precisely be established, in which the practice of torture seemed to stop on the orders of Prime Minister Menachem Begin.

In 1984, I handled an incident which became a landmark, known as 'the Shabak affair' (or 'the affair of bus no. 300'). Related to this affair, it was later disclosed that two kidnappers had been killed by Shabak officers at the orders of the head of the Shabak, after they had been captured. The affair was revealed in 1986, from the ranks of the Shabak itself. In this case the press, which had covered up the Shabak's activities for years, turned its back on the Shabak. Indeed, public awareness grew. Pleas were submitted to the Supreme Court (including mine, on behalf of the victims' family), which failed to deliver justice. This blessed arousal of the public was referred to by the President of Israel and other defenders of the Shabak as the 'dance of the devils', and in order to put an end to it the President decided to pardon the Shabak men.

The cold-blooded murder of two Arabs was not the aspect that constituted the essence of the incident for the authorities or for the judicial establishment. This was stressed by the press, and evident in the court's decision. The human aspect was neglected, while attention was focused on the lies of the Shabak interrogators and their deliberate misleading of committees which had been set to investigate the affair. Indeed, this was an indication of the dehumanization of the Palestinian victims, which reached its climax during the Intifada. However, during the same period of the Intifada a new and welcome phenomenon became manifest: the creation of various human rights organizations which documented the acts of torture and condemned them, initiating a struggle against the practice.

Following 'the affair of bus no. 300', interrogation practices did not change. Tens of prisoners came to me with complaints concerning acts of torture in the Tul-Karem, Jenin, Nablus, Farah and Hebron prisons. These acts of torture included being hung by one's hands on special hooks, being tied to one's chair, starvation, blows to all parts of the body, especially to the genitals, being denied access to a toilet, and sleep deprivation. Abed El Fateh Said complained of being held in solitary confinement and enduring all of the above-mentioned forms of torture, in addition to the fact that his torturers spat in his mouth. We appealed to the Supreme Court in his name, only to have the plea treated with scorn by the state in a similar fashion to the case of Sulaiman Najab and others in 1974, twelve years earlier.

The adage 'time is money' seems to be one of the Shabak's guiding principles. The practice of torture reduces the amount of time necessary to extract a confession and the number of investigators necessary to be placed on a case. For this reason it is useful to install a 'closet'[2] in which the prisoner becomes 'soft' quickly and confesses before he suffocates. According to the accounts of numerous prisoners, this torture device can be found in the Jenin and Hebron prisons and in the Jerusalem jail.

In 1987 an investigative commission, the Landau Commission, was established to examine the 'interrogation methods and procedures of the Shabak in the realm of terrorist activity and in giving testimony in the courts in connection with these interrogations'. The commission was established following the incident of Azat Nafsu, a Druze officer in the Israeli Defence Force, who confessed and was convicted of things he did not do as the result of an illegal investigation by the Shabak. I delivered many complaints to this commission on behalf of my Palestinian clients, including a description of the terrifying closet mentioned above. My clients also complained about interrogators who worked in Gaza Central Prison, in which some detainees actually died during the course of interrogations. No allegations or complaints made by Palestinians were mentioned in the report published by the Landau Commission. The commission commented on the sixteen years of lies told by Shabak personnel (I think there are a few years missing here), but did not specify what these lies intended to cover up. Reflecting upon this discriminatory attitude towards the Palestinian complainants, and the legitimacy given to torture by the Landau Commission through its definition of torture as 'moderate physical pressure', I have no choice but to accuse the commission of racism. The commission's approach in allowing the practice of torture is similar to that of the Spanish Inquisition, which recommended the 'moderate use of torture'.

Maintaining its traditions, the Shabak tortured Awad Chamdan, aged 23, who died in Jenin Prison. Chamdan died while under interrogation on 21 July 1987, two days after his arrest. When arrested, Chamdan had been in a state of complete health. I made a complaint over his death, together with a demand that the Shabak interrogators be investigated by the Landau Commission while it was still active. A short time thereafter it was revealed that the Shabak officers provided the commission with false testimony, claiming that Chamdan had died of natural causes. Thus, before the ink could dry on the commission's recommendations and its determined statement that the Shabak interrogators had returned, after sixteen years of deception, to the essence of truth, it became evident that they had again deceived the commission which had been established, among other reasons, in order to investigate their deceptions.

The 'erroneous' medical report from the pathological institute regarding the cause of Chamdan's death enabled the Shabak interrogators to lead the commission to believe that the prisoner had died of natural causes. A very strange death this was indeed, when at first it was said to be from a snake's bite, later from a heart attack and finally from pneumonia. The true cause of death emerged only after a prolonged legal battle: suffocation. It is a pity that I cannot disclose the manner in which Chamdan was suffocated, which was revealed to me following another plea to the Supreme Court.

For the Shabak, the incident had a 'happy ending'. The interrogator responsible was accused of 'causing death from carelessness', and tried in Jerusalem. He was acquitted on the basis of the benefit of the doubt, in a hearing which was conducted behind closed doors. My insides burst when I, who know that Chamdan died of suffocation at the hands of his interrogators, must keep silent while the court tries a man for 'carelessness'.

Mahmud El Masri's death on 6 March 1989 in the Shabak wing of Gaza Central Prison was another strange death which occurred during interrogation. In December 1989, Haled Camal Sheich Ali died in the same wing. He was not the last.

As a result of our public and legal struggle concerning the deaths of El Matur from Dahariah and El Masri, the right of a family to demand representation by an independent doctor at post-mortems was first recognized. The family members of El Masri had noticed bruises on his body which later were specified by Professor Founder, the independent pathologist, as being twenty-four marks of violence. While the official cause of death had been reported to be the bursting of a stomach ulcer, Professor Founder determined that there was a clear causal connection between the violence that was used against the victim, as indicated by the marks on his body, and the bursting of his stomach ulcer. Moreover, the bursting of the ulcer lasted twenty-four hours, during which the deceased received no medical treatment despite his many complaints. What more needs to occur to elicit examination by a doctor? Spitting blood and twisting from pain to the verge of losing consciousness were not enough to convince the Shabak interrogators that the man was in need of medical assistance.

The Shabak interrogators reported that they were not impressed by complaints of prisoners concerning their medical condition. The Shabak regarded these complaints as a deliberate attempt to avoid interrogation. Nor were they impressed by the decision of a judge who ordered a detainee to be examined by a doctor, as in the case of Mustafa Akawi, who died in Hebron Prison on 4 February 1992. In this incident the military judge revealed indifference, for he did not release a man who complained of violence despite the fact that Akawi exhibited clear indications of having been violently beaten. The judge gave an order that Akawi be examined by a doctor, which the Shabak ignored, choosing instead to continue his subjection to inhumane interrogation which ultimately led to his death.

Indeed, the system works, suffocates and exterminates. Mustafa Barakat from Anbata suffocated from asthma and Aiman Naser from inhaling gas, both 'natural' deaths. Apparently, as in the case of El Masri, the Shabak is allowed to wash its hands clean before a judicial system which is shamefully sympathetic to it. Where are those who see the pain in the eyes and the convulsions in the face? Where are those who hear the screams? Soldiers, prison officers, medics, physicians ... What a terrible thing has happened to us, that we have come so far. Abu-Hani has been succeeded by a second generation of torturers aided by silent assistants and collaborators, and a new generation of vindicators has emerged.

All of Orwell's distorted vocabulary will not be enough to validate the vermin which is called torture. This practice constitutes, among other things, a violation of the Fourth Geneva Convention, which is equivalent to crimes of war. While indeed the perpetrators of war crimes are not always punished for their deeds, there is still a chance that we will be held accountable for the acts which we have committed. On such a day, all the commissions and the various ministers, including the dovish ones, will not be enough to eradicate the disgrace. And the torturers and their collaborators will pay the price for their crime.

Notes

1. Before the beginning of the actual trial that relates directly to the accusations, the defence lawyer can conduct a mini-trial (also known as a *dire voire* trial) in which he or she claims that the confession given by the defendant was extracted under pressure, and therefore cannot be used as evidence.

2. The 'closet' is a narrow receptacle for detention with room only for the prisoner's body and a few holes for breathing.

ROBERT H. KIRSCHNER

International status of medico-legal investigation

The status of medico-legal investigation in many countries is variable, ranging from the virtually nonexistent to highly sophisticated systems in some jurisdictions in North America and Europe. In the United States, there is a mixture of medical examiner and coroner systems. The medical examiner is usually appointed by the local or state governing authority and is a physician with special expertise in forensic pathology. Coroners are usually elected, and there are no requirements that the coroner have any special knowledge or expertise in medico-legal death investigation. In fact, very few coroners are physicians. As a result, they must employ forensic pathologists to perform those autopsies that are deemed necessary. Medical examiners and coroners in the United States investigate not only deaths that occur under suspicious circumstances, but all deaths that occur in custody, deaths that occur in persons previously in a state of health, and deaths that may be related to medical diagnostic or therapeutic misadventures. In virtually all jurisdictions, the medical examiner or coroner is, by statute, independent of the police, courts and prosecutors.

In Western Europe, the laws governing medico-legal death investigation vary. Recently, member countries of the European Community (now Union) have been working to standardize these laws through the Seville Working Party on the Standardization of Medico-Legal Death Investigation. In Europe, medico-legal death investigation is more likely to be associated with a university department of legal medicine or forensic medicine. In the United States, such academic affiliations are unusual. Autopsy rates vary widely from country to country, and in some countries authority to perform an autopsy must come from a judge, who makes decisions on a case-by-case basis. This is unfortunate, since it puts a lay person in the position of deciding whether a medical procedure is necessary, interposes an unnecessary layer of bureaucracy and may bias an investigation.

In many countries of the world there are no qualified personnel capable of performing a proper medico-legal autopsy or even a proper medical autopsy. The scientific investigation of crimes using modern forensic techniques is usually also lacking in such countries. Crimes are solved almost totally by gaining confessions from suspects, and it is not surprising that in such countries torture of criminal suspects is routine. (While torture of political prisoners always gains the most international attention, torture of criminal suspects is much more common and is routine in countries such as Mexico, Turkey and India.)

Because of the disgraceful state of the medico-legal death investigation in so many countries, particularly in cases involving government wrongdoing, it became obvious several years ago that international standards of medico-legal death investigation should be established. A group of attorneys and forensic experts assembled by the Minnesota Lawyers' International Human Rights Committee (now known as the Minnesota Advocates for Human Rights) prepared a manual on the effective prevention and investigation of extra-legal, arbitrary and summary executions. This document was submitted to the United Nations and was ratified in 1990 as an official document of the UN. This manual, which includes a model autopsy protocol and enunciates principles on the effective prevention and investigation of extra-legal, arbitrary and summary executions, now sets an internationally recognized standard for medico-legal death investigation. Most importantly, the principles included within the protocol declare the rights of families to a thorough and impartial investigation of the circumstances of death as an integral part of the investigation. The principles also give the family of the deceased broad rights in obtaining representation at autopsy and access to the results of all autopsy findings and circumstantial evidence.

The medico-legal autopsy

Before proceeding to a discussion of medico-legal death investigation within the State of Israel, it is important to understand that there are two concepts of the forensic autopsy, which to some extent are reflected in the traditions and laws governing forensic pathology in different countries. The first approach to the forensic autopsy is what I call the 'black box' method. In this method, the forensic pathologist performs the autopsy with a minimal amount of outside information. This is done intentionally so that they are not biased by the alleged circumstances of death, but are able to offer an objective description of all the injuries and other physical findings, determining the cause of death based on the types of injuries found upon the body. In such a method, the pathologist gives this information to the police, coroner or judge for further investigation and action. There is no independent investigation of the circumstances of death by the pathologist. Where the cause of death cannot be determined by the autopsy alone, the burden then falls on other investigators to collect the necessary evidence. The manner of death (i.e. natural causes, homicide, accident or suicide) is then determined by the appropriate legal authority, often at an inquest or other public hearing.

In contrast to the 'black box' method, the 'gestalt' method focuses more on the forensic pathologist as the individual to determine not only the cause but also the manner of death. It is the responsibility of the forensic pathologist to gather police reports, medical records and other information and evidence regarding the circumstances of death to help them to make these decisions. This latter approach is appropriate and necessary when death occurs in custody, or other ambiguous circumstances. In such instances information provided by police or military authorities cannot be relied upon as objective or accurate.

The role assigned to the forensic pathologist may be determined by tradition or statute. An independent medico-legal death investigation system in which the forensic pathologist is responsible for determining both cause and manner of death is particularly important when deaths occur in custody, or where other agents of the government are suspected of participating in causing the death of the individual. The United Nations manual on the effective prevention and investigation of extra-legal, arbitrary and summary executions clearly outlines the obligations of all governments to guarantee that such an independent investigation takes place.

The case of Israel

In Israel, the forensic institute at Abu Kabir is under the Ministry of Health and thus theoretically independent of the police and the military. However, the institute operates under the 'black box' method of forensic pathology. Thus, diagnoses are based on the autopsy alone, and only the cause of death is determined. The results of the autopsy are provided to the police or military and are not released to the family. This leads to the situation that we have seen on so many occasions, with Palestinians dying in custody of 'natural causes' and investigation of the circumstances of death clearly showing that these 'natural deaths' – e.g. heart attack, asthma, ruptured ulcer – are precipitated by interrogation methods that fall within international definitions of torture. Deaths precipitated by such forms of interrogation should properly be labelled homicides.

The Institute of Forensic Medicine under the direction of Dr Yehuda Hiss operates in a competent and professional manner. The deficiency in the Israeli system lies in the tradition of isolating the autopsy from the scene and the circumstantial aspects of the death. Medico-legal death investigation in Israel, particularly of deaths in custody, could be improved by expanding the powers and responsibilities of the forensic institute. The following suggestions are offered:

1 Legislation should be introduced in the Knesset to expand the reponsibilities of the Institute of Forensic Medicine. An investigative section should be established within the institute which would have the authority to conduct an independent investigation of all deaths in custody in Israel and the Occupied Territories.

2 The Institute of Forensic Medicine should be given the power to subpoena evidence, police and military reports, and medical records.

3 Autopsy reports should be released directly to families within thirty days of the conclusion of the autopsy.

4 An autopsy should be performed not only in all cases of death in custody but in all cases where death occurs as a result of military or police action, such as shootings. It will require significant effort to convince Palestinians of the advantage to them of such a proposal. (One element of this would be to arrange that bodies be transported in Red Crescent ambulances rather than by the Israeli military.)

5 Continued monitoring by outside observers will provide assurances to the Palestinian population that death investigations are fair and impartial.

11 The modern inquisition state

AVIGDOR FELDMAN

The Landau Commission Report authorized the General Security Services (GSS) to use 'moderate physical pressure' when interrogating those suspected of terrorist activities. The legal significance of this report was the fact that it put an end to Israel's denials and attempts to hide acts of systematic torture. Instead, Israel became a 'modern inquisition state', as evidenced by its candid admission of the employment of torture or its bureaucratic equivalent – moderate physical pressure. In so doing, torture is justified with legitimate objectives. As a consequence of this transition, the status of the GSS was modified from that of a legal spectre that appears in the dark of night in the corridors of bureaucracy and government, into a legitimate and bureaucratic body. The process is not yet complete. The GSS, like H.G. Wells's Invisible Man, is being gradually revealed – here and there a hand, leg or nose emerges, and yet the connection between them remains transparent.

Israeli law does not recognize the GSS. No law established it – it simply came into being, together with the state. Like the state itself, the GSS enjoys a natural status similar to a being or element that belongs to the world of natural phenomena – like birds, wind and water – rather than to the normative, artificial world of the law. According to the law, the head of the GSS has less authority than a meter maid in Tel Aviv. The existence, actions and authority of the GSS are the result of an unwritten system of agreements between it and other state-sanctioned authorities. Such a phenomenon is astounding in a state that regulates all authority and power in a complex system of laws, regulations and mandates. Even though the GSS is the chief interrogator in all security offences in Israel and the Occupied Territories and has, under an agreement with the police, 'first-night rights' with every person suspected of a serious security offence, Jewish or Arab, it has no authority to search, no authority to arrest, no authority for independent investigation. At most, it is authorized by the Chief of Police to interrogate. The GSS is actually mentioned in only four laws. Three of these – the Protection of Privacy Law, the Phone Tap Law and the Criminal Procedures Regulations – grant it powers to invade privacy, tap telephones and postpone meetings between a detainee and a lawyer for up to two weeks, without the legislative body apparently being concerned by the fact that those powers are granted to a body which does not exist under the law. (The fourth law concerns income tax relief for GSS personnel.)

Since the GSS is not regulated by law, its interrogators have no immunity for an action carried out as part of their function. Immunity is granted to a police officer or a Nature Preservation Authority supervisor. It appears that for this reason – according to a leak that was publicized – a Cabinet committee that was recently discussing changes in the Landau Report recommendations sought to grant the GSS the same immunities as those enjoyed by police officers. The recommendation does not appear among those eventually made by the committee, and apparently the GSS relented when it became clear that the price would be the passing of legislation defining the powers and immunities of GSS interrogators.

The total absence of any legal authority has not weakened the GSS. On the contrary, it has allowed it to reside as the violent and parasitic occupant of the covert internal space created at the centre of governmental architecture. It is in this space that illegal interrogations – often involving torture – can be carried out. Legal authority for the actions which are necessary for the execution of the GSS's work – search, arrest, detention – is absorbed from the police, the prison services and the Attorney General's office by a technique of parasitism or 'body snatching'. The GSS has penetrated and taken control from within, like a parasitic organism, of existing and legitimate institutions and organizations, and supports itself by feeding off the powers of the institutions in whose gut it has settled. When a GSS interrogator needs someone arrested, he approaches a police officer and asks them to make the arrest. In most cases the officer does not think twice about the request, nor do they ask for evidence justifying the arrest. The arrest is made and the detainee is handed over to the GSS interrogators, who maintain interrogation and arrest wings in legitimate prisons and detention centres. At one trial, the warden of the Russian Compound detention centre testified that the GSS interrogation wing in the centre operates as an autonomous unit under the absolute control of the GSS. Even in the event that he might see a detainee, who is officially entrusted to his care, with a hood on their head or handcuffed for hours on end – treatment which is a violation of the regulations by which he is to work – it will not even cross his mind to breach the tacit agreement between the police and the GSS. By allowing the detention of prisoners in the 'GSS wing' of legitimate prisons, wardens provide the GSS with prison services. Even the fact that the prisons and the police serve the GSS as contractors for arrest and detention is not regulated in law, but has arisen out of agreements, which nobody stops to think about, between the GSS and the authorities, whose powers are usurped.

When a GSS officer requires the extension of a detainee's arrest, a police officer is dispatched to the court. The police officer has played no role in the investigation and possesses no knowledge of any of its details. The GSS officer provides them with a sealed document that is delivered to the judge, containing the details of the suspected offence and the evidence. The police officer, or in some cases the lawyer, appearing in court is in fact a body without any independent will, and a sharp eye will detect the little hump just below their shoulder blades, the seat of the GSS officer who snatched the body by using his powers. And when the judge leans over and gives the decision for a fifteen-day extension of arrest – based solely on the secret opinion of the GSS, which is shown neither to the detainee nor to their lawyer – it is difficult to determine from the defence table whether the little hump on the judge's back is a crease in their shirt or something else.

The covert internal space within which the GSS operates in the State of Israel, a country which denies its practice of torture, acts to isolate acts of torture from public review, and to isolate the issue of legitimate authority from torture. In this manner, the links between Israel as a democratic state and practices that contradict basic principles of the rule of law are maintained. This can only be achieved by means of a stain on the democratic field of vision, thus preventing the staining and corruption of the democratic institutions and of those in authority, who have continued to provide proper democratic services to the untortured population, and whose functioning has not been tainted by direct exposure to torture. A legitimate administration would aspire to isolate the practitioners of torture from regular authorities, fearing that torture tempts and corrupts, and that anyone who has used it once cannot be trusted not to use it again in situations that threaten the public not naturally a target for torture. Everyone, with the exception of the actual victim of torture, has an interest in the continued existence of the covert internal space, which is the explanation for its strength and endurance for so long a period of time, that is, until the Landau Commission transformed Israel from being a 'denying state' to one resembling an inquisition. In such a regime, torture is bureaucratized. It is given names and euphemisms generally used in legitimate techniques of government and interrogation – the forms, the authority, the permits and licences, the supervision. Especially important to such a system is its commitment to bring to trial those who deviate from the norm, who abuse the limited authority to torture, those who, in the course of the torture, cause irreparable harm or even death. The trial and sanction of the deviators grant those who abide by the guidelines for moderate torture a normative status beyond appeal. This is how torture is normalized, hidden from view. Because replacement of denial with inquisition is not retrogression and the adoption of an old political model; it is a sophisticated transition from hiding and denial by disclosure. Inquisitorial regimes use the principle well known from Edgar Allan Poe's mystery stories, according to which the more a fact is disclosed, the more it is kept out of sight. An inquisitorial regime bureaucratizes the practice of torture in order to hide and insinuate it in between legitimate government techniques.

Israel is at present in the process of making the transition from being a denying state to becoming a modern inquisition state. The covert internal space that has not yet disappeared, even as the bureaucratization of torture is under way, creates new administrative borders. What was once hushed up and silent is now faltering, looking for the proper words for itself, such as 'waiting'. As part of the increased supervision of the GSS, its interrogators are now obliged to keep written memos of interrogations. On the form, the moderate physical pressure is called 'waiting'. Forms given in evidence in courts show extended waiting periods – sometimes ten hours or more. In these waiting periods, according to testimonies of both detainees and warders as provided in court, the detainee sits or stands, a sack is put over their head, and they are tied up painfully. The use of the word 'waiting' has historical etymological roots; in the past, the courts ruled that the head of a person being interrogated can be covered with a sack only while they are waiting to be interrogated, so that other detainees will not recognize them. This permit has been wickedly turned into a permit for the moderate physical pressure exercised, *inter alia*, by the sack over the head of the detainee during long hours of 'waiting'. The word also has a metaphorical meaning; those waiting are actually the interrogators, and while they wait they fall into a deep sleep from which they awaken as if kissed by the handsome prince, only when the detainee has returned from the covert internal space for further legitimate interrogation.

Especially enlightening is the 'medical' form, which was obtained by Advocate Tamar Peleg from the Association of Civil Rights in Israel. It looks like any other government form – heading, items, places for an 'x' with 'delete where inapplicable' – and the physician is required to confirm, in the appropriate place, that the detainee is fit for the exercise of moderate physical pressure.

This ties in with the deep and ironic suggestion of Professor Lion Shelef of Tel Aviv University, that torture should be carried out under the order of a judge who must define the level of torture that the interrogator is permitted to exercise on the detainee, based on the nature of the suspicions against them and the quality of the evidence – just as a judge signs search warrants or arrest orders. Thus there will be an order for a slap, or for moderate squeezing of the testicles. And appeals will certainly be allowed before a district court judge, who will propose that the parties should reach a settlement entailing a good spit in the eye. From the moment that Judge Landau and the other members of the commission rolled up their sleeves and got down to the work of writing the interrogator's manual of moderate physical pressure, which describes the types of physical harm permitted, the inquisition state shook off the dust of history and got to its feet.

The successful operation of an inquisition state requires the total cooperation of numerous authorities which formerly existed outside of the circle of torture in the denying regime. In the inquisition regime, legal counsel, the State Comptroller, the Knesset, the government and the courts are all drawn knowingly and willingly into the torture circle as collaborators. The bureaucratization of torture, which is based on forms, ministry jargon, hierarchy and norms, conceals the personal responsibility for acts of torture. The inquisitorial regime is much more than a denying regime, which is aware of the immorality of torture and devotes efforts to conceal the shameful secret which is hidden in the covert internal space. The arrogance exhibited by the Landau Commission by not giving in to the hypocrisy inherent in the concealment of torture, and exposing what other regimes do out of sight, has caused long-term and profound harm and corruption that far exceed any damage caused by the regime's denials and hypocrisy that preceded the report.

Workshop: possibilities for change through the courts

led by LEA TSEMEL

The struggle in the courtroom against torture has been such that any sense of progress has been inevitably followed by set-backs. This 'victory followed by defeat' scenario is best demonstrated by the Landau Commission Report. In its investigation of the interrogation practices of the General Security Services (GSS), the report made constraints against the practice of certain acts of torture. At the same time, the commission's approval of the use of 'moderate physical pressure' legitimized the continued practice of other 'interrogation techniques' which constitute torture. This frees the Israeli authorities from the need to conceal the practice of torture, which has been judged necessary for the nation's security by the Landau Commission headed by Supreme Court Judge Landau.

The conclusion of the Landau Commission Report and its consequences bear witness to the legal status of torture in Israel. The practice of torture by the GSS has become more difficult to penetrate due to the legal veil established by the commission.

The innovations of the GSS and the state's protection of its activities necessitate a sophistication among those engaged in the fight against the practice of torture, particularly the lawyers who are responsible for representing the defendants in court. The court expects the defending lawyer to provide evidence and prove beyond doubt the claims of the defendant. Even when he or she succeeds, it is in the judge's authority to determine if the defendant was tortured on the basis of his belief in the credibility of the witnesses. Regarding the testimonies of the witnesses, the judge determines their validity on the basis of his own discretion.

There have been countless cases brought against the state involving torture which had good prospects of winning, particularly 'mini-trials' (*dire voire* trials), which were defeated on the basis of technicalities. These technicalities have included minor discrepancies in the testimony provided by the plaintiff, which have allowed the state defence to have them dismissed as untrustworthy. Additionally, minor procedural errors by lawyers not familiar with the particular procedures inherent in such cases have led to the dismissal of the allegations.

As the legal struggle against torture proceeds, it is important that new 'tactics' are developed. Greater openness around interrogation practices must be achieved. This is possible by exposing those involved in all levels of the practice of torture. While the number of 'professional' interrogators who are directly responsible for the torture of detainees may be limited, they are facilitated by a much larger body of people, including soldiers, physicians, medics, prison guards and police officers. These individuals fail to expose what is going on in the prisons, and their duties often include silent assistance in the practice of torture. For example, they are the ones who prevent the prisoners from sleeping and refuse them access to the toilet. By uncovering the identities of these accomplices to torture, they can be called upon to testify in the courts.

Among the more sophisticated and elusive means of practising torture which the GSS has developed is the employment of collaborators. In the past they have been Palestinians convicted of crimes who have agreed to collaborate in exchange for various benefits. More recently their number include political prisoners who have broken under pressure and agreed to cooperate with the GSS. They are employed by the GSS to extract confessions from detainees through a variety of tactics such as posing as members of the Intifada security squad within the prison. Due to the manner in which the Landau Commission limited the use of torture, the GSS has increased its employment of collaborators, using them to carry out torture in its more brutal forms. The collaborators are allowed to stage mock-executions and to violently threaten and beat the interrogatee. The employment of collaborators is also significant because it makes it difficult to pin the responsibility of torture on the GSS or other Israeli authorities. At the same time, the GSS continues to use violent methods such as position abuse, sleep deprivation, deprivation of outside stimuli and food deprivation. The GSS interrogations are recorded and some of them are filmed. Until this day, defence lawyers in Israel have not been allowed to see these recordings, which leads one to suspect that the methods used during interrogation are unlawful. Legal strategies should be developed and employed against these methods.

Proposals for action

1 Efforts must be made to provide prisoners in the Occupied Territories with the same civil rights as those persons arrested in Israel. Present discrepancies concerning the rights of persons in Israel and

the Occupied Territories include the period of time which is allowed to pass before detainees are given the chance to receive legal counsel and appear before a judge – which is eighteen days in the Territories while it is only forty-eight hours in Israel.

2   In comparison with the situation in other countries, the percentage of lawyers involved in the effort to protect human rights is very small in Israel. Attempts should be made to reach lawyers who otherwise work with issues unrelated to torture. In South Africa a programme was established in which such lawyers were given the case of individual political prisoners which they were to follow. Such lawyers, who might normally deal exclusively with matters of taxation or the like, would monitor the proceedings of the case. This proved to be an effective means of informing and involving a greater number of individuals within the legal profession in South Africa in the effort to protect human rights in their country.

3   The media must be better utilized to expose the ongoing practice of abuse and torture in prisons and interrogation centres. The complaints of torture victims should be published. The Israeli public should be made aware of the proceedings of cases concerning the abuses of the GSS. It is imperative that the doors of the court be opened to allow public criticism of the procedures of such trials rather than allowing these cases to proceed behind closed doors, as is usually the case.

4   As the court proceedings involving cases against the GSS become more sophisticated, it is important that the gathering of evidence concerning abuses of torture become more professional. Cases of torture at the hands of the GSS must be acted on immediately so that the most exact evidence possible can be produced, as the smallest discrepancies can render it useless. In this regard, workshops should be arranged to provide training in the gathering of such useful information from the victims of torture which can be later used in cases against the GSS.

5   Attendance at the court proceedings of those trials which are open to the public would be of assistance to the legal struggle against torture. By this means, the atmosphere within the courtroom can be influenced in such a manner that those testifying are made aware of the fact that there are people in Israel who oppose what is happening in the cells controlled by the GSS.

6   The protocols of court proceedings concerning abuses by the GSS are significant instruments which must be used in other trials.

7   In order to ensure that detainees comprehend the proceedings of the case brought against them, confessions made by Palestinians should

also be written in Arabic, and not only Hebrew, as is usually the case.

Note

The workshop was attended by some sixty people from Israel, the Occupied Territories and abroad. Lawyers, health professionals, human rights workers and others were among the participants.

PART IV

Rehabilitation of torture victims

INGE GENEFKE

When discussing and working with torture victims, the issue must be approached from several perspectives. These include: the definition of torture, namely, what are we talking about when we say that someone has been tortured?; epidemiology, namely, how widespread is torture today?; and further questions: what kind of information do we have about the contemporary practice of torture? What is being done to prevent torture and to assist its victims? And what are the needs of the future?

Definition of torture

The definition of torture has been developed over time. When we at the Rehabilitation and Research Center for Torture Victims (Denmark) began our efforts at intervention against the practice of torture and our medical work rehabilitating its victims nearly twenty years ago, the problem of defining torture became apparent to us. We initially employed the definition of torture appearing in the World Medical Association's (WMA) Declaration of Tokyo (see Appendix B), which was adopted by the Twenty-Ninth World Medical Assembly in October 1975. In this Declaration, torture is defined as

> the deliberate, systematic, or wanton infliction of physical or mental suffering by one or more persons acting alone or on the orders of any authority, to force another person to yield information, to make a confession or for any other reason.

Over the years we came to realize that torture must be approached in more refined terms, such as 'government-sanctioned torture', which specifically addresses torture performed with the knowledge and consent of governments. For that reason we are now using the definition of the United Nations Convention against Torture and Other Cruel, Inhuman or Degrading Treatment or Punishment of 1984 as it appears in Article 1:

> any act by which severe pain or suffering, whether physical or mental, is intentionally inflicted on a person for such purposes as obtaining from him or a third person information or a confession, punishing him for an act he or a third person has committed or is suspected of having committed, or

intimidating or coercing him or a third person, or for any reason based on discrimination of any kind, when such pain or suffering is inflicted by or at the instigation of, or with the consent or acquiescence of a public official or other person acting in an official capacity. It does not include pain or suffering arising only from, inherent in or incidental to lawful sanctions.

In addition to this definition, we orient our work according to Article 2 of the same Convention. We believe, above all, that torture should not be allowed in any country. We believe that a command from a superior, whether it be from a government official or from an officer of the security forces, cannot be used as an excuse for practising torture. There is no acceptable excuse whatsoever for any act of torture.

Epidemiology: how widespread is torture today?

According to Amnesty International, government-sanctioned torture is practised in seventy-seven countries – roughly half of the nations in the world. It is important to note that the UN's Convention against Torture has been ratified by only seventy-one governments (as of June 1993). Although we believe that all countries should ratify the UN Convention, we know that such an act is not enough. Israel, for example, ratified the UN Convention against Torture in 1991, and yet the practice of government-sanctioned torture in areas controlled by its security forces has continued.

The contemporary practice of torture

When we began intervening against the practice of torture and rehabilitating its victims we knew little about the dynamics which torture involves. However, through our work we learned much about the nature of the contemporary practice of torture.

One of the initial discoveries we made was that contemporary torture is designed to create after-effects. Like everyone in the early 1970s, we knew that torture was horrible and unbearable when undergone. Yet it came as a surprise to learn that torture involves after-effects – physical as well as psychological. Now it is common knowledge that, after experiencing torture, torture survivors suffer for years from depression, anxiety, a feeling of changed personality, shame, guilt, impaired memory and concentration, headaches, sexual problems, fatigue, etc. We learned that the methods employed by those practising torture were deliberately designed to create such after-effects.

In the 1970s we had thought that the aim of torture was simply to obtain information. However, through our work we learned that the primary aim is to destroy the victim's identity and personality. We observed that the group of individuals targeted for torture are those whom we define as the community's strong personalities: union leaders, politicians, leaders of ethnic minorities, human rights fighters, student leaders, journalists, etc.

These individuals are detained, their identities and personalities destroyed by the torture, and eventually they are returned to their environment. The women and men who entered the torture chamber as leaders later emerge as broken individuals, with their strength removed. Not only are they no longer capable of being leaders, but the very sight of these broken individuals serves as a warning to others in the community. This provides dictators and repressive regimes with an effective tool for the suppression of a society. In this light, we have discovered that torture is the most destructive force against the further development of democracy.

Torture as a process and a method

Torture begins with the arrest. The arrest usually takes place at night with a formidable display of power and an unnecessary use of violence. The 'softening phase' which often follows usually consists of a few days and nights of unsystematic violence and humiliation. This is usually followed by systematic acts of torture in which the torturers explore the victim for their weak spots, which are later exploited.

The torturers avoid breaking down their victims too quickly. Were they interested in breaking down their victims within a short period of time, they would typically utilize well-known techniques. The victims are placed against a wall and beaten. Each time they fall over they are beaten so as to get up again. They are denied food or water. They are hooded. They are denied access to the toilet. They are exposed to constant and loud noise.

A few days of such suffering induces a state of confusion which is sometimes accompanied by hallucination. People subjected to this form of torture who are broken down quickly are actually easier for us to help than those who have fought against such torture for days, weeks and months until they finally break down and sign statements, giving names, false evidence, etc. Such individuals feel that their soul has been broken to pieces. This, of course, is well known to the torturers.

The result is an individual stripped of self-respect. The same authorities who have broken the victim's personality may also have supplied him or her with a false medical certificate denying any form of maltreatment. The end result may also be death, in which case the torturers will typically dispose of the corpses in an unmarked mass grave.

Methods of systematic torture can be divided into physical and psychological forms, usually performed simultaneously. The intention of the systematic methods is that the physical and psychological destruction of the victim will continue into the future. Contemporary sophisticated torture methods are constructed in such a manner that, while they destroy the identity and self-respect of human beings, the torturers can claim that the victims were never exposed to torture. In many countries, torture is practised with the assistance of psychological and medical professionals. In fact, a new science has been developed.

The methods of physical torture are varied. They can include the application of electric shocks to the most sensitive areas of the body; the suspension of the victim by an arm or by a leg, which can last for hours; the immersion of the victim's head under water until the point of suffocation; the burning of the victim's skin with cigarettes or red-hot iron rods; beatings aimed at specific parts of the body, such as under the feet until the soles are badly damaged. Sexual abuse is common, particularly against women, though men are also sometimes harmed in their ability to function as men; dogs can be trained to rape both men and women. Sanitary conditions in detention are usually extremely poor, any request for visiting the toilet becoming a pretext for torture; the victim is kept alive with filthy food and drinking water; freedom of movement is limited, with prisoners often packed so closely as to force them to sleep in turns.

Physical torture is complemented by acts of psychological torture. Methods such as sleep deprivation, blindfolding and isolation invoke a deep sensation of fear and helplessness and can also provoke hallucinations. Total isolation can be maintained for years, in which time the victim is uncertain of their fate, and their family is ignorant of their condition and whereabouts. Many victims are coerced to say or do things which violate their ideology or religious convictions, the purpose of which is to destroy fundamental parts of the victim's identity related to their self-respect and self-esteem. Political and ethical values are attacked by techniques such as the coercion to sing songs which praise the very things which the victim is against. Mock-executions lead the individual from a sense of reality into a nightmarish state of almost suspended animation.

The breaking down of the victim's personality begins with their arrest. Names are replaced with numbers. Personal belongings are removed, including glasses, life-saving drugs, etc., and are replaced with ill-fitting uniforms.

The effect of torture

Torture has been developed in such a manner that it creates conditions which effectively strip the victim of their personality and identity, destroying their ability to lead a normal life among other human beings. The worst consequences for the survivors of torture are psychological. The period of torture is often followed by profound feelings of guilt and shame which can result from the victim's mere survival while friends may have died under torture; or they result from the thought that information the victim supplied could have harmed friends. An example of a technique known to produce such deep feelings of guilt is the so-called 'impossible choice', a situation in which the victim is forced to make a choice between, for example, revealing the names of their friends or seeing family members tortured. Regardless of which choice the victim makes, the result is a disaster for which they feel responsible, which is exactly the aim of the torturer.

Psychological studies performed at the Rehabilitation and Research Center for Torture Victims (RCT) involving the survivors of torture frequently reveal the following symptoms: anxiety, memory loss, depression, changed personality, disturbances affecting memory and concentration, and nightmares about the prisons and torture. Fatigue, headache and sexual disturbances are also common.

Where the psychological after-effects of torture can be considered to be the same in all torture survivors, the physical after-effects depend on the torture methods used. Falanga (beating of the soles of the feet) results in impaired walking; suspension by the arms results in shoulder pain; and so on.

As barbaric and horrible as these descriptions might sound, we have discovered that the survivors of torture can in fact be rehabilitated. When we know what they have been through, it would seem as though a miracle is necessary for them to recover. But they can be rehabilitated, which is the task we undertake at RCT. It is important to note that the after-effects which follow torture are normal reactions from healthy individuals.

Survivors of torture from forty-six countries around the globe have been rehabilitated at RCT. Our experience has taught us that the methods of torture are the same all over the world, which is a direct reflection of the fact that the objectives and goals of the torturers are also similar. The after-effects are the same, and consequently the rehabilitation is the same (of course, one should observe cultural differences).

The myth of silence surrounding torture has been broken. We are there to speak on behalf of the tortured. We, and not the survivors themselves, will tell of their torture, their feelings of isolation, shame, guilt, depression, etc. We have broken the myth. We have penetrated behind the torturers.

Though mere doctors of medicine, we could also conclude, through social analysis, that the practice of torture is the most destructive force against democracy. We conducted research which led to further knowledge. Today we can state the following concerning the diagnosis of government-sanctioned torture:

— As mentioned earlier, at the individual level, we have found that the victims of torture are usually the 'strong personalities' in the community: leaders of ethnic minorities, fighters for human rights, union leaders, politicians, student leaders, journalists, etc.
— Concerning the trauma, we find that government-sanctioned torture is performed in seventy-seven known countries, and in these countries imprisonment most often includes torture. Further, through our discussions with the survivors of torture we can analyse, on the one hand, the relationship between methods of torture and the after-effects exhibited by the victim, and, on the other hand, the coping mechanisms which they display.
— Concerning the examination of the torture survivors after imprisonment, we now know more about the physical and psychological symptoms and objective findings.

Thus, as far as the diagnosis of government-sanctioned torture is concerned, we can state that we have determined a reasonably well-defined group which is at risk; a reasonably well-defined list of trauma; and a reasonably well-defined list of physical and psychological symptoms and objective findings. We can, with a high degree of certainty, state whether or not a person has been exposed to government-sanctioned torture.

What is being done to prevent torture and assist its victims?

The medical work against torture focuses on rehabilitation, education, research, documentation and the implementation of ethical codes and conventions against torture. The work is performed by health professionals: medical doctors, psychologists, nurses, social workers, physiotherapists, etc. Centres have been established, or initiatives have been taken to establish centres, in fifty countries around the world. Several of these countries have more than one centre. The International Rehabilitation Council for Torture Victims has contacts in 111 countries.

It should be stressed that we are capable of rehabilitating torture survivors. We can diagnose government-sanctioned torture, and based on our social analysis we know that government-sanctioned torture is the most destructive power against democracy. Thus, we possess a weapon against government-sanctioned torture: we know how to diagnose; we are able to rehabilitate; and we have a global network to do so.

What are the needs of the future?

The significance of our ability to diagnose government-sanctioned torture must be reiterated, as it represents an important weapon against repressive regimes. Governments can attempt to deny their practice of torture, but we are able to prove its existence. With the professional knowledge which we possess today, we believe that it might be possible to abolish government-sanctioned torture before the year 2000.

Our future work has several aims. We are striving to fortify our global network. We are working to improve our work with rehabilitation, education, research and documentation. We want to be able to further implement ethical codes and conventions against torture in different countries around the world. Additionally, we aim to increase the general awareness of the ongoing practice of torture, which itself is important, but also to be able to increase the financial resources available to our work. We believe that members of the United Nations should give a very high priority to the UN Voluntary Fund for Torture Victims. It presently has a tiny budget of $1.6 million, which is shameful in light of the need. We believe that members of the United Nations are obligated to make a significant increase to this budget.

In conclusion, it is appropriate to quote a few sentences from David Grossman's moving book, *Yellow Wind* (1988):

> I wanted to meet the people, those who in fact are the pawns in this dramatic game, those who are the first to pay the price for their actions and mistakes, courage, cowardice, corruption, nobleness. I soon realized that we all pay the price – but we are not all aware of it.

This is true not only for Israel – it is true for the entire world. We all pay the price for the ongoing practice of torture. Many of us are simply not aware of it.

Torture and mental health: a survey of
the experience of Palestinians in Israeli prisons

EYAD EL-SARRAJ

Since the Israeli occupation of the West Bank and Gaza Strip in
1967, around 400,000 Palestinians have been detained or imprisoned.
Reports of torture perpetrated by Israeli interrogators are now common
knowledge and have been documented by international organizations
such as Amnesty International as well as by Palestinian and Israeli
human rights groups. Sadly, however, the Israeli governments have
persisted in allowing the use of torture. In June 1992 the International
Committee of the Red Cross publicly expressed its condemnation of
the Israeli treatment of Palestinian prisoners. All to no avail.

Aware of the increasing number of clients suffering from various
syndromes and pathologies which are related to their experience of
being tortured, we decided to conduct a survey on the extent of torture
and its effects on mental health. In an environment of widespread
suspicion, tension and fear, it was not an easy task to accomplish.

Methodology

To design the questionnaire, we first approached fifty ex-political
prisoners. We asked each to describe their experience from the moment
of arrest, through interrogation and imprisonment or detention. In the
light of our clinical experience with victims of torture, we then designed
a questionnaire which included the following items:

1   Personal details, age, sex, area, marital status.
2   Methods of physical torture.
3   Methods of psychological torture.
4   Subjection of family members to ill-treatment.
5   Methods of arrest.
6   Total period in prison.
7   Frequency of imprisonment.
8   Harassment after release.
9   Health problems during imprisonment.
10   Difficulties in adjustment following release.
11   PTSD (post-traumatic stress disorder) check-list.

A sample of 700 ex-political prisoners were asked to participate by our trained fieldworkers, themselves ex-political prisoners. We tried to include all geographic areas of the Gaza Strip and all political factions. In order to cover the short- and long-term effects of torture, we included people who had spent between six months and ten years in prison or detention.

Around 200 of those asked to participate in the survey refused to do so. Some did not feel totally safe and feared retribution. Others felt that it was pointless to produce more reports, in the belief that it will help neither them nor others.

Results

Results indicate that wide-ranging methods of psychological and physical ill-treatment are employed against prisoners in order to force their admission to the charges placed against them.

A large majority of the subjects were tortured by:

Beating	95.8%
Extreme cold	92.9%
Extreme heat	76.7%
Prolonged periods of standing	91.6%
Application of pressure to the neck	68.1%
Deprivation of food	77.4%
Solitary confinement	86.0%
Sleep deprivation	71.5%
Intense noise	81.6%
Verbal humiliation	94.8%
Threats against personal safety	90.6%
Forced witnessing of torture of others	70.2%
Pressure applied to testicles	66.0%

Other methods to which prisoners were subject:

Irritant gas	13.4%
Instruments placed inside penis and/or rectum	11.1%
Electric shock	5.9%

The survey also revealed the ill-treatment of members of prisoners' families by Israeli soldiers. This ill-treatment included:

Beating of family members	44.9%
Destruction of private property during arrest	31.0%
Torture of family members in their presence	28.1%
Threats that their wives or mothers would be raped	27.9%

The survey indicates that, following the period of incarceration, the victims of torture experience difficulties readjusting to normal life:

Difficulty adapting to family life	41.9%
Difficulty socializing	44.7%
Sexual and marital problems	20.1%
Economic difficulties	76.5%

All of the participants were asked to answer a check-list of PTSD symptoms. Results show that 29.1 per cent have more than eight symptoms which indicate the need for psychiatric intervention.

Conclusion

The Israeli employment of systematic torture against Palestinian prisoners has clearly damaged thousands of individuals and has seriously affected the social fabric of Palestinian society. As concluded by our study, 29.14 per cent of the sample are exhibiting psychiatric symptoms. In addition, 44.7 per cent of the sample have expressed their difficulty in resuming normal socialization. Evidently, this is due to their feelings of suspicion and paranoia. Many of these people are convinced that collaborators with the Israeli authorities are everywhere, and they have lost trust in the people around them.

We claim that a large proportion of the Palestinian population is suffering from the direct effects of torture and that the whole society is indirectly affected. We are concerned about the perpetuation of the cycle of violence, the well-being of every victim of torture and the effects of victimization on the psychological make-up of the Palestinian people.

For the present situation to be improved, concerted efforts on different levels are required. Efforts at intervention are necessary to bring the systematic practice of torture by the Israeli security forces to an end. In the case of the rehabilitation of torture victims, such efforts constitute 'preventive medicine'. Palestinian and Israeli human rights organizations must work in cooperation to achieve a mainstream demand for the reform and monitoring of Israeli interrogation practices to meet the international agreements of which Israel is actually a signatory. Success in this endeavour would be a major step towards breaking the cycle of violence which characterizes life in the Occupied Territories.

Significant efforts are necessary in order to heal the wounds, both physical and psychological, of the survivors of torture. Rehabilitation centres must be built and qualified personnel trained to deal with the trauma that Palestinians have suffered in Israeli prisons. This process of healing must also include the indirect victims of torture, first and foremost the family members of those who have been tortured.

A necessary and often overlooked aspect of the rehabilitative process is the question of monetary compensation for the torture victim. It is important for such compensation to be made, both as a means to provide funding for the rehabilitation process, and as an acknowledgement of the wrongs committed by Israeli security personnel.

14 Compensation suits as an instrument in the rehabilitation of tortured people

NEVE GORDON

The process of rehabilitation for a tortured person must deal with more than mere psychotherapy and medical treatment – it must also include consideration towards their existential situation: the relationship with their family, their social and occupational environment, and the political realm in which they reside. I believe that most people agree that by continuously addressing the practice of torture through the court system we can have some impact on stopping its use. Taking both of these factors into account, we at the Association of Israeli-Palestinian Physicians for Human Rights (PHR) found that compensation suits can be used as an effective tool in the struggle against the practice of torture in Israel and can simultaneously be an organic element in the rehabilitative process of the individual who has endured torture.

PHR has recently taken part in the filing of two suits against the State of Israel and the General Security Services (Shabak), claiming compensation for damages caused as a result of torture. To the best of our knowledge these are the first and only two compensation suits pertaining to torture that have ever been submitted to the Israeli court. We believe that the act in which a tortured person sues those responsible for the torture inflicted is in fact a struggle for justice.

The Israeli legal system
The military courts aside, the Israeli judicial system can be roughly divided into two spheres: civil and criminal law. In a case involving allegations of torture, one can choose between criminal proceedings or the filing of a compensation suit according to civil law. It must be noted that these legal actions do not contradict each other and can be utilized simultaneously. In order to understand the advantages of submitting a compensation suit I will give a brief outline of both the civil and criminal procedures.

Criminal proceedings

According to Israeli criminal law, a person who has been tortured can choose between two courses of action: to file a complaint to the police or to file a direct criminal complaint to the court.[1] Once a complaint is filed and the police have concluded the investigation, the material is passed either to the Attorney General or to the Police Attorney. If there is adequate implicating evidence and it is found to be in the 'public interest', an indictment is submitted to the court and the proceedings begin. If the State Attorney decides against filing an indictment, for reasons of either insufficient evidence or lack of public interest, then the complainant has the right to appeal to the Government Legal Adviser. In any case, the complainant always has the option to submit a direct criminal complaint to the court. However, even if a direct criminal complaint has been submitted to the court, according to the law, the Attorney General at any time in the proceedings has the right to take the case from the hands of the complainant and assume the role of the prosecutor. Thus, even in a direct criminal complaint, the complainant does not have control over the proceedings. Another aspect of criminal proceedings which is relevant to our topic is the fact that the accusations in such proceedings must be against specific people, for example a certain Shabak interrogator, and not against the state or its institutions.

Filing a complaint to the police regarding a criminal offence is the right of every person, even if they are not directly connected with the offence. Thus, for example, PHR can file a complaint to the police describing the torture inflicted upon Mr Omar Jaber, and, as stated in clause 59 of the criminal law, the police are compelled to open an investigation.

Investigation of torture allegations

PHR has sent numerous complaints of torture to the Ministry of Police demanding an investigation. However, the Israeli police does not investigate the Shabak but, rather, passes the complaint to the Attorney General, who in turn passes the complaint to the Shabak's department of internal investigations. This procedure is in open contradiction to Israeli law, which states very clearly that it is the responsibility of the police to investigate all criminal offences. Furthermore, when a body is allowed to investigate its own actions it distorts all correct procedures. Nevertheless, the norm determines the proceedings, and the horrible fact is that the Shabak is allowed to investigate itself.[2]

The Shabak's department of internal investigations investigates the complaint and returns it to the Attorney General. We have no knowledge of what the investigation constitutes, nor can we know if the material gathered during the investigation is actually passed to the Attorney General. All we know is that the complainant, in many cases PHR, receives a laconic answer from the Attorney General, usually stating that the events described have been investigated, and that the Shabak officer acted in accordance with regulations.

Civil suits

In cases involving permanent or temporary damage of a physical or mental nature caused by torture, a compensation suit can be filed. The acts relevant to torture for which one can be sued are assault, mistaken imprisonment and negligence. It should be noted that torture, as a legal term, does not appear in Israeli law. Unlike the criminal suit, the civil suit can be directed against both the interrogators and the state or its institutions, as the employer or sender of the sued person.[3]

In cases where the employer is found to be negligent, it can then be convicted, whereas in instances of assault the state is responsible only if it ratifies the assault. In such cases the employee is still responsible. For example, in its answer to our suit pertaining to Hassan Zbeidi, the state responded that the 'interrogators did not assault Mr Zbeidi and if they did, we, the State, do not ratify the act since we do not permit assault'. Therefore, the tendency when submitting a civil suit is to avoid basing it solely upon accusations of government-sanctioned assault, since all the state needs to claim is that it does not sanction the assault. In the case of Mr Zbeidi, for instance, where we do not know the names of the interrogators, we chose to establish our accusations on state negligence. The legal distinction between negligence and assault is that an assault is considered intentional while negligence is not.

Seldom would we choose mistaken imprisonment as the fundamental accusation on which to base a civil compensation suit, as the detainee is usually held in accordance with the law or in accordance with some kind of military regulation. Only if the lawyer finds a technical fault in the legality of the imprisonment would it be worthwhile to emphasize the accusation of mistaken imprisonment.

Nevertheless, we choose to accuse the defendant of assault, mistaken imprisonment and even the practice of torture, but of all of the acts against which we are suing, it is negligence that gives us the best chance of winning. Israeli law defines negligence as the deviation from reasonable behavioural norms. When suing for negligence in cases where torture was practised, we are essentially stating that the Shabak interrogator did not act in the manner an interrogator should act.[4]

Civil suits versus criminal proceedings

The advantages of civil suits over criminal proceedings can be analysed on two different levels: from a legal perspective and a rehabilitative one. Interestingly enough, there is a close correlation between the two.

Control over the proceedings

The proceedings of a civil suit are controlled by the person who was harmed, in this case the tortured, while in criminal proceedings the State Attorney has the prerogative to take over the case at any time. Let me reiterate; in the civil suit the tortured is the initiator of the suit, responsible for directing the strategy of the proceedings, and even has the power to withdraw from the suit. By contrast, control over the proceedings in a criminal case is usually in the hands of the State Attorney, and even in cases where a direct complaint is submitted to the court it can be taken from the hands of the tortured at any point.

Mere awareness of their control over the situation helps people who have been tortured to emerge from the status of victim and regain their dignity. Conversely, lack of control over the proceedings can reinforce the feeling of being a victim. More than that, the deep frustration that so often accompanies legal struggles of this kind creates the possibility of regression in the condition of the tortured. The potential to stop and withdraw from the proceedings is very important to the tortured, and should be emphasized to them along the way.

Furthermore, there is a metaphorical substitution of the roles of those involved, which at times helps the tortured person overcome some of their fears and anxieties. The interrogator and his employer become the defendant; they have to answer to the court; and they become the ones with something to lose. Most important, they are no longer omnipotent; they are no longer in full control of the situation; they are vulnerable, and the tortured person sees them in this condition. The former victim also knows that they are now the one responsible for the uncomfortable situation of their former oppressors.

The opportunity to compromise

The opportunity to compromise expresses the control which the complainant has in civil suits, and also lays bare another essential difference in the proceedings themselves.

Civil suits are much more open to compromise than criminal suits. During the proceedings of compensation suits, it often becomes clear that the question of guilt is actually the question of quality and quantity of guilt. How much guilt the defendant is willing to take upon himself (if at all) is reached through an agreement between the two sides. In civil suits the tortured person takes part in the negotiations and decides whether to agree to the suggested compromise. It is not only the feeling of control over the negotiations and the decision that is significant to the tortured, but also the fact that they must cope with the concept of agreement.

Criminal proceedings do not allow the same room for compromise, often determining the procedure by an either/or verdict – guilty or not-guilty. Even when there is some kind of settlement in criminal suits, it is negotiated between the state and the defendant, while the complainant does not really have a say in the agreement. Our experience has taught us that, in cases where security officers are involved, settlements between the prosecutor and defendant are made in bad faith – the defendant gets off lightly – which only reinforces the tortured person's perception of being in a dead-end situation.

Compromises usually shorten the legal process, and provide some kind of tangible results within a reasonable period of time. It is not enough that justice be done – it must be done quickly. Although it is clear that compensation cannot provide the tortured with full justice, it does create a feeling of accomplishment and can contribute to their rehabilitation. By contrast, when a legal suit is dragged out in the court for years, it leads to a general feeling of frustration which prevents the wounds from healing.

The degree of proof

To win a conviction in a criminal suit, the prosecutor must convince the court that the defendant is guilty beyond all reasonable doubt. The probability of guilt in a criminal case must therefore be very high. In a civil suit, the degree of proof is the extent of balance in the probability of guilt; namely, that it is more probable that the events happened than that they did not happen.[5]

It is clear that the lower probability of guilt needed in compensation suits objectively raises the chances of winning the suit. The concept of success, particularly in a struggle against the torturer, is very important, due to its close relation to justice. A major step in the healing process is that the great injustice which has been inflicted upon the tortured person be corrected. Success in a suit leaves the tortured with the feeling that some measure of justice has been served – not only served but witnessed before the court. This feeling can help them achieve reconciliation with themselves and their milieu.

Suing the state

Suing the state broadens the effects of civil suits and often provides the opportunity to raise matters of principle that cannot be addressed in criminal cases. The incentive for raising accusations against the state can range from a desire to attain a larger amount of money, to promoting the political struggle against the practice of torture. PHR thinks that all of these motives are worthy, but we try to emphasize the significance of the political struggle to the tortured person. Through the raising of accusations against the state, the suit has a larger impact on the struggle against torture. By becoming part of this struggle, the tortured person often transcends the sphere of personal responsibility and enters the public realm. We feel that this political responsibility is a significant step in the rehabilitation process, because through it the tortured person feels that they are a member of society, and not in a position of isolation. They support society, and society supports them.

Disclosure of documents

In civil suits each party must disclose all of the documents in its possession,[6] while in criminal suits only the prosecution is required to disclose its documents. Furthermore, in criminal suits the state as prosecutor is not obligated to reveal the documents it gathered concerning the tortured person or complainant. All of the criminal complaints pertaining to the use of torture by Shabak personnel that were sent by PHR to the Attorney General were dismissed under the claims that the evidence was not conclusive or that the allegations were found to be false. Never during our six years of activity have we seen any documentation pertaining to an investigation of our complaints. Furthermore, more than once the tortured person for whom we filed a complaint was threatened by Shabak personnel to the point where they signed an affidavit denying any allegations of torture.

When suing the Shabak or any secret police, there is usually limited proof of torture other than the permanent damage to the victim. If there is no permanent damage as a result of the torture, and there is no documentation indicating that torture was used, then the proceedings will be based on the Shabak's word against the tortured person's word – a situation providing little chance for success.

As already stated, both sides are obligated to disclose their documents in a civil suit. The prosecutor is able to lay hands on documents from the Shabak and perhaps find papers that will support the tortured person's claim. In Hassan Zbeidi's case, we received significant information from the disclosed documents. We learned from his medical report of 9 September 1992 that he was examined upon arrest and found healthy by a prison medic; that on 15 October he was transferred to the emergency room in Tel Hashomer Hospital by the prison doctor; and that on 28 October he was released in a catatonic state by a reserve doctor at Farah Prison. Only due to the civil suit were we able to receive the medical reports from the time of his detention and learn that Mr Zbeidi was arrested in good medical condition and released in a catatonic state.

The disclosure of documents not only benefits the legal sphere, but also has significance for the rehabilitation process. As light is shed on the truth, the tortured person's version is strengthened. The feeling that their word no longer stands alone against the institutions of the state – that what they endured was at least partially documented and has become common knowledge – strengthens their self-esteem.

Compensation

The struggle to obtain compensation is a positive process for the tortured person to engage in, although I think it is often accompanied by adverse side effects. One such side effect is the motivation for a tortured person not to become healthy until the end of the proceedings. This is a complex situation in which it is in the tortured person's interest to maintain their sickness or disability in order to substantiate their victimization and in that manner win the struggle against the torturer. In this sense, the possibility of compensation can at times impede the transition from victim to survivor which is essential for rehabilitation. For this reason, a compromise which can result in a quicker settlement is further advantageous.

The monetary compensation gained is important for different reasons. Primarily, it symbolizes the victory of the tortured over the torturer, playing an important therapeutic part in the rehabilitative process. Additionally, by gaining compensation the tortured person partially loses the feeling of dependency.

When survivors of torture receive compensation for their suffering, it not only helps their personal situation but is significant for the state in which they were tortured. I believe that once Israel pays compensation to a tortured person the state will begin a self-rehabilitating process. Indeed, once money is passed to several tortured people Israel will be admitting that it has tortured, that it is responsible for the torture and that it is responsible for the rehabilitation of the victims. It will take responsibility according to Article 14 of the UN Convention against Torture, which it ratified in 1991. The article states that 'Each State Party shall ensure in its legal system that the victim of an act of torture obtains redress and has an enforceable right to fair and adequate compensation including the means for as full rehabilitation as possible.'[7]

In conclusion, when one compares criminal proceedings with civil suits it seems clear that within the Israeli legal context compensation suits are a useful tool to fight torture and can become an organic part of the process of rehabilitation. I believe that they might well be the best tool we have for bringing about some measure of justice in the case of people who have been made to suffer torture. I will suggest to those of you living in countries with a similar legal system to adopt the use of compensation suits as a means of struggle.

Notes

I would like to thank Attorney Dan Assan for his guidance and assistance throughout the writing of this chapter.

1. Israeli law differentiates between three categories of offences – 'sin', 'offence' and 'crime' – for which a person can be sentenced to from six months' to more than three years' imprisonment. In cases of criminal complaints that do not fall under the category of 'crime' – more than three years' imprisonment – the police have the right not to open an investigation, on the grounds of a lack of public interest. Since allegations of torture fall under the 'crime' category, the police are compelled to open an investigation.

2. It should be noted that in the past Shabak interrogators have been convicted and even sentenced to imprisonment. These have been very few – there is no record of the actual number – but nevertheless the irrational fact that none of the complaints made by PHR led to a conviction teaches us much about the process of enquiry.

3. Israeli civil law, clause 7, states that a civil servant cannot be convicted if he or she acted in accordance with the regulations. The employee's belief that their action was in accordance with regulations is sufficient for them not to be convicted. The employer, in our case the state, cannot be convicted if the act was in accordance with the law and in the case of specific injustice – thus, the employer cannot be convicted when an employee acts in contradiction of regulations.

4. This approach is not politically correct, since what we are in fact stating is that we know the Shabak regularly beats people during interrogation, but in this specific case the interrogator did not follow the regulations and for that reason he caused damage. In other words, the Shabak interrogator left marks on the interrogated person, and therefore he is guilty.

5. The probability of guilt required in a criminal case ranges between 90 and 100 per cent, while in a compensation suit it is only 51 per cent.

6. In both criminal and civil proceedings, the state executes a 'Defence Ministry immunity' on any document that bears the slightest smell of the secret services. The court cannot accept any document that has been defined as immune by the Defence Minister, even if the prosecutor already has the document.

Defence Ministry immunity can be fought in the Supreme Court. The court will be asked to determine if the interest of security supersedes the interest of justice.

7. United Nations Convention against Torture and Other Cruel, Inhuman or Degrading Treatment or Punishment, 1984, Article 14.

15 The Medical Foundation and its commitment to human rights and rehabilitation

HELEN BAMBER

A human rights commitment

The Medical Foundation for the Care of Victims of Torture[1] sees torture as a social, political and moral problem that arises on coordinates in terms of time and geography which are frequently planned as a political strategy at local and global levels. Whenever it is applied on a systematic basis, torture has historical precedents and well-designed social consequences. In these cases it is usually associated with other major features of political instability, and the individual sequelae of torture are therefore often difficult to disentangle from trauma associated with other man-made calamities like warfare, political conquest, dispossession and exile in a foreign land. Meaningful progress in rehabilitative work with survivors requires an understanding by all concerned that such work is part of a broader human rights commitment addressing these issues.

Since our inception we have worked to establish a model of care and treatment which we believe to be appropriate to the special needs of our clients. Through a combination of medicine, casework and a range of psychological, social and physical therapies, we aim to encompass the needs of the whole person. By integrating self-help principles with the specialist services of a multi-professional team, we have found that almost all our clients can be helped in some way to overcome problems that are frequently severe and sometimes apparently intractable.

Our clients include people from some sixty-five different countries whose experience of violence may be as recent as yesterday or as remote as World War II. Since the organization's inception in 1986, refugees and asylum seekers have been seen for brief or extended help. We currently have 7,000 clients on our records, of whom about 1,000, including new referrals, are seen in any one year.

A commitment to rehabilitation with individuals and families

Many of those we see have suffered extensive physical trauma. In these and in other cases of torture, there may be massive psychic trauma which, if unattended, will almost certainly be compounded rather than alleviated in time. We work according to the principle of positive intervention through medical attention and through sustained and structured emotional support in all those cases where people express a need that allows us to engage with them in constructive terms.

In all those cases in which physical trauma is implicated, the principle of positive intervention begins with a medical consultation. The physician conducts a sensitive medical examination in which the principal therapeutic factor is one of engagement rather than imposition. We find that this plays a part in legitimizing help-seeking behaviour across a wide range of cultures. Furthermore, as a specialist in physical disorder, the physician has a direct and practical role to play, as well as an indirect symbolic one, in helping restore to individuals the privacy and integrity of their own bodily processes. The separation of body from mind is nowhere less appropriate than in the treatment of torture, where the body has been abused to gain access to the mind. An integrated physical and psychosocial approach is developed from this basic principle of positive intervention involving the combined endeavours of a multi-professional team.

The concept of cure is in many cases inappropriate. Such post-traumatic sequelae are not the conditions of an illness so much as a form of bondage through which the torturer ensures that his interventions will last over time. The rehabilitative aim is centred on the purpose of freeing victims rather than curing them. Damage is in many cases profound and extensive, but in almost all that come to our attention there is something constructive to be done. (See the case studies below to illustrate this point.)

An organizational commitment

Separate individual treatments and discrete, unrelated resources are less useful than the resources of a team. Survivors' feelings of grief, rage and helplessness need a containing environment where staff can accept and work with them.

A young man spoke of the process of 'decompensation', the abreaction of profound trauma, not long after arriving in London from his home in Central America, where he had been tortured and had seen others suffer. Until he was seen at the Medical Foundation some months later, there was no one who could encompass the terms of his anguish. And so, he told us, 'the forest was my doctor'. He would visit a patch of beechwood nearby where he would run about, cry and shout in great distress, relieving pent-up emotions. The Medical Foundation, he was later to say, 'took over from the forest'. Survivors need a relationship with a community rather than with a specific treatment, and only in a therapeutic community can staff feel sufficiently supported by one another to endure repeated exposure to extreme experience.

Survival as a creative act

People's responses to stress are influenced by their own appraisal of the situation and their capacities to process the experience, to attach meaning to it and to incorporate it in their belief systems. Resilience in adversity is not only a strategy for coping but a creative challenge. People's developmental histories, cognitive set, affectional base, relationship network and prior experience of mastery and self-confidence through challenge and adaptation are determining factors in their reactions to massive trauma. In the range of therapies offered, we have found it essential to make contact with people's prior forms of adjustment and to reactivate internal and adaptive stategies for further recovery.

We have been profoundly impressed by the dignity of those who survive torture and by the importance they attach to transcending the victim identity and to reacquiring a sense of agency and creative endeavour in their lives. We have come to regard the services as aids for the sometimes remarkable powers of self-renewal that our clients bring to us. Ordinary social relationships contain those agencies for change which can, when tapped, release profound self-healing, regenerative resources. We see our professional skills as a means towards this end.

One of our clients, incarcerated in the Middle East after serious injuries under torture, comforted a friend whom he had watched being hurt. 'Old man,' he said, 'we cannot strike them back now. I cannot save you. But while we are here in prison I shall teach you to read and write and that will be our victory over them.' He had been a teacher and so by teaching others he found himself able to survive and to maintain his dignity. Group therapy conducted in the Medical Foundation played an important role in his subsequent rehabilitation, for it helped him rediscover strengths and resources in himself which he believed had been irrevocably destroyed. He had lost most of what he loved and valued, and a sense of inconsolable loss pervaded the other features of post-traumatic stress from which he suffered. Above all, he felt he had lost himself. 'I no longer know who I am.'

Through the dynamics of the group process he discovered that he had not lost the capacity to be of use to others and was finally able to understand the true value of his action in sustaining his fellow prisoners in the face of such immense catastrophe. On this discovery he began to rebuild his life.

Survival as a process of bearing witness

Disaster imposes a sense of isolation on each survivor. The reduction of this isolation must be a central part of the process of recovery if people are to make genuine adjustments. The sustained and structured emotional support available at the Medical Foundation has the aim of sharing with survivors acceptance that they have witnessed disaster of incomprehensible magnitude. Many come to see that the testimony they provide in the process of bearing witness carries a responsibility towards the past, which is one of the keys towards adjustment in the future. This can become one of the most powerful antidotes to the guilt of survival; and the telling of stories, the recounting of narrative, has become an integral and engaging aspect of the Medical Foundation's life.

Torture as a secular inquisition

Torture has always been an instrument of war. It is today also the means for maintaining a particular kind of 'peace'; and to achieve social control through coercion or terror, the state has established itself as a contemporary secular inquisition in many countries. The suffering of the individual is thus the torturer's access to the community. The victims of torture are always individuals, but never individuals alone. For every person detained, there are mothers and fathers and wives and children who wait. Torturers deprive the community of its individuals. Just as significantly, they deprive the individual of community by attacking the trust and coherence which make the fabric of any society.

Torture as a perverted form of intimacy

Torture frequently involves an intimate and intense relationship between an individual and one or several others. The body and mind of the victim are a focus for concentrated attention, either in the form of an onslaught or assault, or in a process which is sustained over time and repeatedly applied. Injury thus arises in a direct and personal relationship, whose purpose is the deliberate destruction of bodily and psychic integrity. Where the body is the primary site of attack, it is the torturer's point of access to the victim's identity and mind. Every physical scar has an emotional scar.

As a personal and intimate violation, the torture process 'borrows' from the prototype of a healing relationship between a person and their doctor, confessor or counsellor. But in doing so it perverts the benign intentions of the healing relationship to induce the very state from which the healer is committed to free their patient.

Racial and other prejudice

Man is capable of torturing fellow human beings, but he feels the need to justify what he is doing. It seems to be a pre-condition for torture that the torturer has a world-view, no matter how crude, that places the tortured into a different category. This distinction can be based on any of the manifold ways of distinguishing one person from another: colour, nationality, class or differing beliefs, usually political or religious. The torturer represents, and by the act of torture is defending, what he believes to be 'good' values. The victim is one who is not in the 'accepted' category. They are not seen as sharing the same humanity.

It is a very basic human tendency to differentiate people into members of in-groups and out-groups, into 'us' and 'them'. Most cultures come to develop strong stereotypes, exaggerated beliefs about the characteristics of a group, or images, frequently devaluative, of some groups of people. Children acquire these stereotypes and de-valuative images. Such differentiations, once made, lead to devaluation of members of the out-group relative to the in-group and to dis-crimination against out-group members.

Devaluation makes it easier to harm people, given that a motivation or reason exists for doing so. Intense devaluation may by itself generate the desire to harm.

A sharp differentiation between one's own group and another group and intense devaluation of the latter not only limit caring and empathy for members of the other group but also exclude them from the range of applicability of moral values. Through devaluation and other pro-cesses, some groups are excluded from the moral universe. It then becomes possible to harm and even to kill their members.

Devaluation of potential victims always occurs before a society begins to purge a group. In Nazi Germany, as in other countries, victims were dehumanized to make them easier to hurt; Jews, Gypsies and others were described as 'vermin' by their torturers.

Devaluation can vary in nature and intensity. In Argentina, the greater the devaluation of victims the more ferociously they were tortured. Communists were regarded as the most direct enemy, while Jews were the subject of intense anti-Semitism. Both were especially cruelly tortured.[2]

In some cases the perpetrator tortures a known victim. In other cases the victim is dehumanized, becomes an object to be used or abused, a non-person who is reduced to a howling animal. This is achieved by a variety of means which include:

— depriving the victim of name and identity (substituting a number), stripping naked, shaving the head or covering the face so that the victim appears as an anonymous member of the targeted group;

— inflicting the maximum degradation on the victim; denying facilities for hygiene, forcing the victim to lie in excrement, leaving festering wounds untreated, etc., with the result of reinforcing the torturer's assumption that the victim is a mere digit in a subhuman category.

Talking of the field tortures he witnessed in Vietnam, an American veteran said:

> It wasn't like they were humans. We were conditioned to believe this was for the good of the nation, the good of our country, and anything we did was okay. And when you shot someone you didn't think you were shooting at a human. They were a Gook or a Commie, and it was okay.

What we perceive is bound to be only partial, since it is informed only by our own experience, some of which has the quality of conditioning. Unless something happens that causes us to review our perceptions, we tend to think, believe and act on assumptions which are largely taken for granted.

Prejudice is no single person's fault; we cannot help the way we and our institutions are conditioned. In consequence, we all make subjective assumptions about groups of people outside our own circle, particularly about those from other national, ethnic or religious groups. If the system of prejudice against out-groups is not interrupted and reversed, it is self-reinforcing. Our task is to question our assumptions. Blame lies only in refusal to do anything to unlearn racism, once we have understood it.

Case studies
Case 1

A young man arrived in London, after a complicated series of moves between various countries, and was living with family friends. He had been held in prison for some three years after his initial detention and torture and owed his escape and freedom to an accident.

Until his imprisonment at about 20 years of age, he was physically robust and problem-free in psychological terms. He was a sports enthusiast, played football and had had a firm and healthy relationship with a young woman whom he hoped to marry.

We found him anorexic, significantly below his optimal weight, incapacitated by a poorly healed fracture to one wrist and by soft tissue damage to the soles of his feet, which had been systematically beaten and deliberately cut by glass. Walking any distance presented a problem.

He suffered from recurrent headaches, a disordered sleeping pattern and morbid ruminations. Exploration of traumatic associations aggravated a tremor which produced a dramatic convulsion for which he had been taken to several hospital casualty departments, where, despite intensive investigations, no neurological or other organic cause could be found.

This was his story: On being arrested he was blindfolded and thrown into a cell. When his blindfold was removed he saw that he was sharing a cell with a former friend, who had obviously been tortured and whose toes had been severed. He was later taken to a small room. Three plainclothes men were present. The walls and floor were bloodstained. There was broken glass on the floor.

He was stripped naked, his hands and feet were bound, and he was hung upside down from a bar on the ceiling with a rope around his feet. The torturers beat him with wire cable and cut the soles of his feet with glass pieces. They burnt him with lighted cigarettes between his fingers and on the backs of his hands. A bloodstained blanket was stuffed in his mouth to prevent his cries. At a later point urine was passed in his mouth, he was punched in the mouth, six teeth were broken and were pulled out with a pair of pliers. Twenty-four hours later he was subjected to a mock-execution. Together with five other prisoners, he was tied to a pole and blindfolded, and when the shots rang out he alone was left alive. He was then locked up in the back of a van with the corpses.

There are events in the course of human conduct to which, as witnesses, the only appropriate responses can be the silence of respect or the indignation of tears. In our work at the Medical Foundation, testimony of this kind is in no way unrepresentative. We are still very often speechless or distressed.

Work with this man began with a detailed history by one of our examining doctors and a caseworker. A great deal of time was spent establishing a relationship of familiarity, and when we were confident he would not experience medical investigation as further bodily intrusion, further neurological tests were performed in the presence of the caseworker he had come to trust. He was seen by a physiotherapist and osteopath for treatment to his feet and to his wrist, and for breathing and relaxation exercises. Staff secured for him a special set of shoes with built-up soles which reduced the discomfort of walking and they also found him a bicycle. Although a relatively minor intervention, this access to mobility was immensely empowering for him and was the beginning of his transition from the role of victim to survivor.

He began a course of individual psychotherapy with the assistance of a translator who was one of his family friends. The translator became part of the treatment process and continued the dialogue outside the Medical Foundation, but in consultation with, and under supervision of, the psychotherapist and caseworker.

Priority in the sessions was given to establishing a convivial and trusting relationship. Close attention was given to his family history, his early life and the period prior to detention. Only six months into his therapy were the details of his torture explored, at which point there was a reccurrence – as we anticipated – of the convulsive seizure described above. Working together with the translator, a routine was established by which, when this occurred, our client was firmly held and massaged on those muscle sites which had gone into spasm. While this was being done, the subject matter which had provoked the seizure was kept under discussion. The assistance of friends and family was engaged to sustain this sort of response at home. During the session he and his therapist turned increasingly towards an exploration of the symbolic content of his vivid and tormented dreams.

Much later in the sessions, when he had learnt enough English to attend without the translator, he would pass a large dictionary backwards and forwards between himself and the therapist. It became a transitional object, a bridge by which to cross from his experience in the past to his experience now in the present.

It was at this time that he was able to enter the painful process of mourning his loved ones who had died under torture or who had been executed.

As is so often the case, he was deeply rooted and 'stuck' in the images of their grotesque deaths, unable to visualize his friends as they had been in the past and unable to move beyond those images. Thus the use of the word 'bondage' with reference to the torturer begins to have meaning. With the help of the caseworker and therapist the young man was able to reconstruct those images to incorporate the wholeness of his loved ones, tracing their lives, their appearance, their laughter, their irritating mannerisms, until in being able to mourn his loss and, so to speak, 'bury the dead' he visualized each one as a whole person and not only in the manner of their dying.

He made slow, consistent progress, evidenced by changes in his mood and his sleeping and eating patterns. His aversion to hot food, the consequence of, amongst other things, years of cold diet in prison, steadily diminished, and he was able to begin eating solids after some dental reconstruction. We knew he was getting better when his weight went up, when narrative about imprisonment no longer produced seizures and when he was able to join a long-term therapy group, joke about an interest in women and use our staff to begin planning a study programme.

Case 2   *Marital and family therapy in the course of protection work and long-term rehabilitation*

A protection agency referred to us, for documentation, a man whose initial application for political asylum in the United Kingdom had been turned down. On our investigating his case to produce verification of his torture experience for protection purposes, major psychological and relationship problems came to light. In addition, a diffuse range of somatic complaints were associated with the bodily sites that had been injured but which were now, in physical terms, entirely well.

Medical investigation was, as an essential routine, a way of clearing the path towards a psychological exploration of the problem. The man's face, injured when he had been forced through a window by his torturers, and a site around the kidney where he had been stabbed, radiated pain for which investigations could not find a physical basis. His level of unresolved grief came to the surface early in explorations in which his wife joined us. Only through her description of her overeating did their maladaptive collusion to protect one another come to light.

He had never been able to share with her the pain of what he had seen and suffered whilst in prison. He wished to protect her from this but was, at the same time, desperately in need of her understanding and presence in the internal world of his memories and losses. He drank to diminish the pain of this conflict.

She wished to protect him from the loneliness and fear she had lived through when he disappeared and there was no evidence if he was dead or alive. She had become depressed and could not eat. Now, to keep those associations 'at bay' she overate.

Their daughter's anxiety state reflected the level of unacknowledged conflict and unhappiness at home. But she was most reluctant, at 11 years of age, to join in the sessions. Our translator, a crucial member in these sessions, helped to frame a formulation by which an examination of the family's history was compared to an investigation of a 'haunted house' in which, by opening all the cupboards and looking under beds, one could prove to oneself that there were no more ghosts.

The daughter entered these discussions in this spirit with relish and humour. Their drinking and eating problems were translated into their own psychological language and, as they learnt to be open with one another, the situation changed dramatically. When the couple, seen on their own, were able to experience and share the pain from which they had been protecting each other, the husband's somatic symptoms were fully resolved and the question of eating and drinking became one for humour and teasing, rather than shame and privacy.

In both case studies it will be seen that the therapist and caseworker were adaptive in their approach, incorporating translators and friends in the therapeutic process and in giving symbolic meaning to objects, such as the dictionary and bicycle in Case 1.

A game was played out in Case 2, enabling the child to dispel secrets which had previously prevented healthy relationships within the family. Even though these secrets were hard for her to hear, she was relieved of the burden of uncertainty and no longer felt rejected by her parents.

It is beyond the scope of this chapter to describe in detail the variety of different facilities that are available to the people who attend the Medical Foundation, people from many different cultures and backgrounds, who are unique as individuals and whose needs must be assessed in the light of their uniqueness.

Our services range from conventional medicine, psychiatry, psychotherapy, family and child therapy, to those complementary therapies which respond to the needs of people whose physical symptoms need to be addressed before they feel able to verbalize their psychological pain. Physiotherapy, osteopathy, movement, art therapy, reflexology, massage and instruction in relaxation methods are important in this context.

The Medical Foundation's work is carried out by both a core paid staff of twenty-eight and a loyal and dedicated volunteer staff who give their time, their skill and their concern to our work as a free gift, and without whom our work would be greatly diminished both in quantity and, above all, in range and quality.

All members of staff, paid or volunteer, have the benefit of personal supervision with a peer supervisor, to discuss and work through the pressures and difficulties of repeating encounters with extreme experiences. Regular clinical meetings, seminars and workshops provide in-house training and support. Many staff attend outside training courses to improve their skills and gain additional professional qualificatons. A staff group, facilitated by two group supervisors, provides the opportunity for all staff to explore their working relationships with each other.

Rehabilitation models

In designing appropriate rehabilitation models, careful assessment must be made of the environment, i.e. the political and economic situation, existing health services, the location of torture survivors in relation to treatment facilities, and the strength of the community in which a rehabilitation programme is to be undertaken.

The Medical Foundation has established from its projects in Uganda,[3] and in other countries with records of torture, that the needs of torture survivors who remain in their own country differ in a number of important ways from the requirements of those who have sought refuge in alien lands.

In response to traumatized asylum seekers and refugees, rehabilitation and psychosocial centres have developed in a number of European cities and in Australia, Canada and the United States. These centres have taken on board the need to provide a rehabilitative milieu that is responsive, not only to the trauma of torture and organized violence, but also to the additional trauma of exile and loss.

A refugee is someone who is forced to flee, to live in an alien and often hostile society. He or she is likely to live in poverty, often in total isolation, deprived of their language, family and friends, with little hope of work and uncertain as to the future. Refugees are dominated by feelings of guilt at having fled, and a painful, traumatic and deep sense of loss, loss of what is obvious, tangible and external and a loss that is less obvious, a loss of personal identity and purpose. Above all, they are deprived of community.

The trauma and needs of survivors who are living in their own country are different. They continue to live in the difficult and dangerous situation in which they were tortured and may be tortured again. However, a person requiring treatment following torture is likely to turn for help to services which are already in place in the community. He or she is less likely to be able or willing to travel to a specifically designated institution or specialist centre which may be in a distant location. Therefore, while the specialist centre may serve the needs of torture survivors who are in exile, it should not be assumed that it is the appropriate model for treating those still within their own communities.

In certain countries where torture is practised, a torture treatment centre could be appropriate where large numbers of survivors are located in a central area. Where torture and degradation are widespread, a single centre treating a small number of individuals fails to meet the needs of the majority of survivors. What is needed in such cases is the enabling of the community to understand the needs of its injured members and to provide the healing support required for their rehabilitation. For the health worker, it is important to remember that our patient is not necessarily 'ill' but, rather, reacting normally to an abnormal situation. Once key members of the community have acquired the necessary expertise, they are able to set in motion a process which enables the community to address the needs of torture survivors.

In order to achieve appropriate rehabilitative help for the greatest number of torture survivors in their own countries, I believe, therefore, that the international community might be best advised to invest its financial resources in the training of local health and community personnel. The survivor would then be appropriately supported in their own community.

There is a further danger attendant on the creation of a centralized 'treatment centre' in each of an increasing number of countries whose governments practise torture. The danger is that in the eyes of the international community the existence of large numbers of such centres could serve spuriously to 'normalize', even to sanitize, the perpetration of criminal violations against helpless individuals. The existence of a multiplicity of such centres must not be allowed to distract the international community into thinking that the problem of torture is being adequately addressed. As in other areas of medicine, rehabilitation is a poor second best to prevention.

The widespread practice of torture, the 'normalization' of torture, not only destroys the victims, but it contaminates the society which practises it by turning populations into bystanders, and some bystanders into perpetrators. Rehabilitation can address some of the needs of a minority of survivors, but the global effect of torture requires other measures.

The duty of every individual working to help torture victims is, first and foremost, to influence and educate society in order to ensure that such abominations become utterly unacceptable both to societies themselves and to the international community, so that any society practising torture becomes an international pariah.

Notes

Some of the material contained in this chapter arises out of joint work with John Schlapobersky, psychotherapist, group analyst and supervisor at the Medical Foundation, to whom I am indebted, and with whom I have collaborated in the production of earlier papers.

1. The Medical Foundation for the Care of Victims of Torture is a London-based independent charity. It was founded in December 1985 to continue work first carried out by volunteer practitioners under the auspices of the British Medical Group of Amnesty International. The organization works to relieve the physical, social and psychological suffering of individuals and their families who have been subjected to torture and other forms of organized violence.

As well as its direct clinical responsibilities, the Medical Foundation has come to play an important national and international role in the documentation and verification of torture, in providing education and publicity about the problem worldwide, and in consultation with, and providing advice to, other agencies and personnel.

2. E. Stanb, 'Psychology and torture', in P. Suedfeld (ed.), *Psychology and Torture*, New York, Hemisphere, 1990.

3. Patrick J. Bracken, Joan E. Ciller and Stella Kabaganda, 'Helping victims of violence in Uganda', *Medicine and War*, vol. 8, 1992, pp. 155–63.

Workshop: processes and questions involved in establishing a rehabilitation centre

led by SOREN BOJHOLM

The workshop began with a presentation of the treatment model and the principles of treatment of torture victims which characterize rehabilitative work of the Rehabilitation and Research Center for Torture Victims (RCT). RCT employs a multidisciplinary approach, including psychotherapy (as the cornerstone), physiotherapy and social counselling, as nearly all torture survivors have experienced injuries to their bodies as well as to their souls. If the torture survivor is living in Denmark, the spouse and children are also offered examination and treatment.

While RCT's experience in the treatment of torture survivors indicates that most physical complaints are psychosomatic, it is nonetheless emphasized that each client must be offered a careful medical examination. The physical examination helps the psychotherapist establish a trusting relationship with the client, and failure to perform the physical examination can create a negative frame of mind for the client, who might not understand how talking can cure a disease.

Within the workshop group itself, the question of rehabilitation and treatment of torture victims was approached from diverse perspectives which reflected the membership of the group. There was broad consensus that the rehabilitation of Palestinian survivors of torture had to be approached in the broader context of a society which has experienced widespread devastation as a result of institutionalized violence, both within and outside of the detention system.

In that respect, the scope of the treatment provided cannot be limited to the victim themselves. The social institutions which are the mainstays of support, particularly the family, are often themselves in a state of devastation and in need of rehabilitative attention. Treatment of a torture victim's spouse and children is necessary, both for their own sake and in order for them to be able to provide support for the survivor of torture.

There are at present a few Palestinian rehabilitation programmes for the victims of violence which exist in a state of isolation from one another. Neither do they have contact with the international community or with Israeli professionals. Members of the workshop group expressed frustration with so-called 'humanitarian tourism', in which international 'experts' come for brief, isolated visits without providing a significant constructive response to existing programmes.

Proposals for action

1 Research: (a) the number of people in need of such services must be assessed; (b) the facilities required to provide these services must be determined; (c) there must be an evaluation of the quality of existing facilities and the means by which they can be integrated into a comprehensive rehabilitation network.

2 Greater communication and coordination among the existing facilities must be arranged.

3 The specific treatment and rehabilitation approaches viable for the Palestinian context must be determined.

4 Training, both for professionals and for volunteers from the community, must be arranged. There was broad consensus that the ultimate purpose of the training programmes must be the education of local people, who can then train other local people. The assistance of international organizations can be significant to this end, provided such assistance takes place on the basis of continued, regular contact.

5 Public education and outreach concerning the results to be expected from torture and ill-treatment could be facilitated by such training programmes. This is relevant in light of the fact that, despite the existence of manuals alerting Palestinians regarding what to do when imprisoned or when their home is raided, etc., there are few resources for what to do after they have actually survived such an experience.

6 Israeli professionals with significant expertise in the area of rehabilitation can be of assistance in three ways: (a) assisting in the training of Palestinian rehabilitation staff; (b) support for campaigns against the participation of health professionals in the practice of torture; assistance towards the prevention of torture helps render rehabilitation less necessary; (c) provision of expert testimony before the courts in cases of abuse.

Note

The participants in the workshop included physicians, a number of Palestinians involved in rehabilitation projects, some human rights workers, and academics. As well as Israelis and Palestinians, there was broad international representation.

International declarations concerning torture

1 Convention against Torture and Other Cruel, Inhuman or Degrading Treatment or Punishment

Adopted by the United Nations General Assembly on 10 December 1984 (Resolution 39/46)

The States Parties to this Convention,

Considering that, in accordance with the principles proclaimed in the Charter of the United Nations, recognition of the equal and inalienable rights of all members of the human family is the foundation of freedom, justice and peace in the world,

Recognizing that those rights derive from the inherent dignity of the human person,

Considering the obligation of States under the Charter, in particular article 55, to promote universal respect for, and observance of, human rights and fundamental freedoms,

Having regard to article 5 of the Universal Declaration of Human Rights and article 7 of the International Convention on Civil and Political Rights, both of which provide that no one shall be subjected to torture or to cruel, inhuman or degrading treatment or punishment,

Having regard also to the Declaration on the Protection of All Persons from Being Subjected to Torture and Other Cruel, Inhuman or Degrading Treatment or Punishemnt, adopted by the General Assembly on 9 December 1975,

Desiring to make more effective the struggle against torture and other cruel, inhuman or degrading treatment or punishment throughout the world,

Have agreed as follows:

PART I

Article 1

1. For the purposes of this Convention, the term 'torture' means any act by which severe pain or suffering, whether physical or mental, is intentionally inflicted on a person for such purposes as obtaining from him or a third person information or a confession, punishing him for an act he or a third person has committed or is suspected of having committed, or intimidating or coercing him or a third person, or for any reason based on discrimination of any kind, when such pain or suffering is inflicted by or at the instigation of or with the consent or acquiescence of a public official or other person acting in an official capacity. It does not include pain or suffering arising only from, inherent in or incidental to lawful sanctions.

2. This article is without prejudice to any international instrument or national legislation which does or may contain provisions of wider application.

Article 2

1. Each State Party shall take effective legislative, administrative, judicial or other measures to prevent acts of torture in any territory under its jurisdiction.

2. No exceptional circumstances whatsoever, whether a state of war or a threat of war, internal political instability or any other public emergency, may be invoked as a justification of torture.

Article 3

1. No State Party shall expel, return ('refouler') or extradite a person to another State where there are substantial grounds for believing that he would be in danger of being subjected to torture.

2. For the purpose of determining whether there are such grounds, the competent authorities shall take into account all relevant considerations including, where applicable, the existence in the State concerned of a consistent pattern of gross, flagrant or mass violations of human rights.

Article 4

1. Each State Party shall ensure that all acts of torture are offences under its criminal law. The same shall apply to an attempt to commit torture and to an act by any person which constitutes complicity or participation in torture.

2. Each State Party shall make these offences punishable by appropriate penalties which take into account their grave nature.

Article 5

1. Each State Party shall take such measures as may be necessary to establish its jurisdiction over the offences referred to in article 4 in the following cases:

(a) When the offences are committed in any territory under its jurisdiction or on board a ship or aircraft registered in that State;

(b) When the alleged offender is a national of that State;

(c) When the victim is a national of that State and considers it appropriate.

2. Each State Party shall likewise take such measures as may be necessary to establish its jurisdiction over such offences in cases where the alleged offender is present in any territory under its jurisdiction and it does not extradite him pursuant to article 8 to any of the States mentioned in the paragraph 1 of this article.

3. This Convention does not exclude any criminal jurisdiction exercised in accordance with internal law.

Article 6

1. Upon being satisfied, after an examination of information available to it, that the circumstances so warrant, any State Party in whose territory a person alleged to have committed any offence referred to in Article 4 is present shall take him into custody or take other legal measures to ensure his presence. The custody and other legal measures shall be as provided in the law of that State but may be continued only for such time as is necessary to enable any criminal or extradition proceedings to be instituted.

2. Such State shall immediately make a preliminary inquiry into the facts.

3. Any person in custody pursuant to paragraph 1 of this article shall be assisted in communicating immediately with the nearest appropriate representative of the State of which he is a national, or, if he is a stateless person, with the representative of the State where he usually resides.

4. When a State, pursuant to this article, has taken a person into custody, it shall immediately notify the States referred to in article 5, paragraph 1, of the fact that such person is in custody and of the circumstances which warrant his detention. The State which makes the preliminary inquiry contemplated in paragraph 2 of this article shall promptly report its findings to the said States and shall indicate whether it intends to exercise jurisdiction.

Article 7

1. The State Party in the territory under whose jurisdiction a person alleged to have committed any offence referred to in article 4 is found shall in the cases contemplated in article 5, if it does not extradite him, submit the case to its competent authorities for the purpose of prosecution.

2. These authorities shall take their decision in the same manner as in the case of any ordinary offence of a serious nature under the law of that State. In cases referred to in article 5, paragraph 2, the standards of evidence required for prosecution and conviction shall in no way be less stringent than those which apply in the cases referred to in article 5, paragraph 1.

3. Any person regarding whom proceedings are brought in connection with any of the offences referred to in article 4 shall be guaranteed fair treatment at all stages of the proceedings.

Article 8

1. The offences referred to in article 4 shall be deemed to be included as extraditable offences in any extradition treaty existing between States Parties. States Parties undertake to include such offences as extraditable offences in every extradition treaty to be concluded between them.

2. If a State Party which makes extradition conditional on the existence of a treaty receives a request for extradition from another State Party with which it has no extradition treaty, it may consider this Convention as the legal basis for the extradition in respect of such offences. Extradition shall be subject to the other conditions provided by the law of the requested State.

3. States Parties which do not make extradition conditional on the existence of a treaty shall recognize such offences as extraditable offences between themselves subject to the conditions provided by the law of the requested State.

4. Such offences shall be treated, for the purposes of extradition between States Parties, as if they had been committed not only in the place in which they occurred but also in the territories of the States required to establish their jurisdiction in accordance with article 5, paragraph 1.

Article 9

1. States Parties shall afford one another the greatest measure of assistance

in connection with criminal proceedings brought in respect of any of the offences referred to in article 4, including the supply of all evidence at their disposal necessary for the proceedings.

2. States Parties shall carry out their obligations under paragraph 1 of this article in conformity with any treaties on mutual judicial assistance that may exist between them.

Article 10

1. Each State Party shall ensure that education and information regarding the prohibition against torture are fully included in the training of law enforcement personnel, civil or military, medical personnel, public officials and other persons who may be involved in the custody, interrogation or treatment of any individual subjected to any form of arrest, detention or imprisonment.

2. Each State Party shall include this prohibition in the rules or instructions issued in regard to the duties and functions of any such persons.

Article 11

Each State Party shall keep under systematic review interrogation rules, instructions, methods and practices as well as arrangements for the custody and treatment of persons subjected to any form of arrest, detention or imprisonment in any territory under its jurisdiction, with a view to preventing any cases of torture.

Article 12

Each State Party shall ensure that its competent authorities proceed to a prompt and impartial investigation, wherever there is reasonable ground to believe that an act of torture has been committed in any territory under its jurisdiction.

Article 13

Each State Party shall ensure that any individual who alleges he has been subjected to torture in any territory under its jurisdiction has the right to complain to, and to have his case promptly and impartially examined by, its competent authorities. Steps shall be taken to ensure that the complainant and witnesses are protected against all ill-treatment or intimidation as a consequence of his complaint or any evidence given.

Article 14

1. Each State Party shall ensure in its legal system that the victim of an act of torture obtains redress and has an enforceable right to fair and adequate compensation, including the means for as full rehabilitation as possible. In the event of the death of the victim as a result of an act of torture, his dependants shall be entitled to compensation.

2. Nothing in this article shall affect any right of the victim or other persons to compensation which may exist under national law.

Article 15

Each State Party shall ensure that any statement which is established to have been made as a result of torture shall not be invoked as evidence in any proceedings, except against a person accused of torture as evidence that the statement was made.

Article 16

1. Each State Party shall undertake to prevent in any territory under its jurisdiction other acts of cruel, inhuman or degrading treatment or punishment which do not amount to torture as defined in article 1, when such acts are committed by or at the instigation of or with the consent or acquiescence of a public official or other person acting in an official capacity. In particular, the obligations contained in articles 10, 11, 12 and 13 shall apply with the substitution for references to torture of references to other forms of cruel, inhuman or degrading treatment or punishment.

2. The provisions of this Convention are without prejudice to the provisions of any other international instrument or national law which prohibits cruel, inhuman or degrading treatment or punishment or which relates to extradition or expulsion.

PART II

Article 17

1. There shall be established a Committee against Torture (hereinafter referred to as the Committee) which shall carry out the functions hereinafter provided. The Committee shall consist of ten experts of high moral standing and recognized competence in the field of human rights, who shall serve in their personal capacity. The experts shall be elected by the States Parties, consideration being given to equitable geographical distribution and to the usefulness of the participation of some persons having legal experience.

2. The members of the Committee shall be elected by secret ballot from a list of persons nominated by States Parties. Each State Party may nominate one person from among its own nationals. State Parties shall bear in mind the usefulness of nominating persons who are also members of the Human Rights Committee established under the International Covenant on Civil and Political Rights and who are willing to serve on the Committee against Torture.

3. Elections of the members of the Committee shall be held at biennial meetings of States Parties convened by the Secretary-General of the United Nations. At those meetings, for which two thirds of the States Parties shall constitute a quorum, the persons elected to the Committee shall be those who obtain the largest number of votes and an absolute majority of the votes of the representatives of States Parties present and voting.

4. The initial election shall be held no later than six months after the date of the entry into force of this Convention. At least four months before the date of each election, the Secretary-General of the United Nations shall address a letter to the States Parties inviting them to submit their nominations within

three months. The Secretary-General shall prepare a list in alphabetical order of all persons thus nominated, indicating the States Parties which have nominated them, and shall submit it to the States Parties.

5. The members of the Committee shall be elected for a term of four years. They shall be eligible for re-election if renominated. However, the term of five of the members elected at the first election shall expire at the end of two years; immediately after the first election the names of these five members shall be chosen by lot by the chairman of the meeting referred to in paragraph 3 of this article.

6. If a member of the Committee dies or resigns or for any other cause can no longer perform his Committee duties, the State Party which nominated him shall appoint another expert from among its nationals to serve for the remainder of his term, subject to the approval of the majority of the States Parties. The approval shall be considered given unless half or more of the States Parties respond negatively within six weeks after having been informed by the Secretary-General of the United Nations of the proposed appointment.

7. States Parties shall be responsible for the expenses of the members of the Committee while they are in performance of Committee duties.

Article 18

1. The Committee shall elect its officers for a term of two years. They may be re-elected.

2. The Committee shall establish its own rules of procedure, but these rules shall provide, inter alia, that:

(a) Six members constitute a quorum;

(b) Decisions of the Committee shall be made by a majority vote of the members present.

3. The Secretary-General of the United Nations shall provide the necessary staff and facilities for the effective performance of the functions of the Committee under this Convention.

4. The Secretary-General of the United Nations shall convene the initial meeting of the Committee. After its initial meeting, the Committee shall meet at such times as shall be provided in its rules of procedure.

5. The States Parties shall be responsible for expenses incurred in connection with the holding of meetings of the States Parties and of the Committee, including reimbursement to the United Nations for any expenses, such as the cost of staff and facilities, incurred by the United Nations pursuant to paragraph 3 of this article.

Article 19

1. The States Parties shall submit to the Committee, through the Secretary-General of the United Nations, reports on the measures they have taken to give effect to their undertakings under this Convention for the State Party concerned. Thereafter the States Parties shall submit supplementary reports every four years on any new measures taken and such other reports as the Committee may request.

2. The Secretary-General of the United Nations shall transmit the reports to all States Parties.

3. Each report shall be considered by the Committee, which may make such general comments on the report as it may consider appropriate and shall forward these to the State Party concerned. That State Party may respond with any observations it chooses to the Committee.

4. The Committee may, at its discretion, decide to include any comments made by it in accordance with paragraph 3 of this article, together with the observations thereon received from the State Party concerned, in its annual report made in accordance with article 24. If so requested by the State Party concerned, the Committee may also include a copy of the report submitted under paragraph 1 of this article.

Article 20

1. If the Committee receives reliable information which appears to it to contain well-founded indications that torture is being systematically practised in the territory of a State Party, the Committee shall invite that State Party to co-operate in the examination of the information and to this end to submit observations with regard to the information concerned.

2. Taking into account any observations which may have been submitted by the State Party concerned, as well as any other relevant information available to it, the Committee may, if it decides that this is warranted, designate one or more of its members to make a confidential inquiry and to report to the Committee urgently.

3. If an inquiry is made in accordance with paragraph 2 of this article, the Committee shall seek the co-operation of the State Party concerned. In agreement with that State Party, such an inquiry may include a visit to its territory.

4. After examining the findings of its member or members submitted in accordance with paragraph 2 of this article, the Committee shall transmit these findings to the State Party concerned together with any comments or suggestions which seem appropriate in view of the situation.

5. All the proceedings of the Committee referred to in paragraphs 1 to 4 of this article shall be confidential, and at all stages of the proceedings the co-operation of the State Party shall be sought. After such proceedings have been completed with regard to an inquiry made in accordance with paragraph 2, the Committee may, after consultations with the State Party concerned, decide to include a summary account of the results of the proceedings in its annual report made in accordance with article 24.

Article 21

1. A State Party to this Convention may at any time declare under this article that it recognizes the competence of the Committee to receive and consider communications to the effect that a State Party claims that another State Party is not fulfilling its obligations under this Convention. Such communications may be received and considered according to the procedures laid down in this article only if submitted by a State Party which has made a

declaration recognizing in regard to itself the competence of the Committee. No communication shall be dealt with by the Committee under this article if it concerns a State Party which has not made such a declaration. Communications received under this article shall be dealt with in accordance with the following procedure:

(a) If a State Party considers that another State Party is not giving effect to the provisions of this Convention, it may, by written communication, bring the matter to the attention of that State Party. Within three months after the receipt of the communication the receiving State shall afford the State which sent the communication an explanation or any other statement in writing clarifying the matter, which should include, to the extent possible and pertinent, reference to domestic procedures and remedies taken, pending or available in the matter;

(b) If the matter is not adjusted to the satisfaction of both States Parties concerned within six months after the receipt by the receiving State of the initial communication, either State shall have the right to refer the matter to the Committee, by notice given to the Committee and to the other State;

(c) The Committee shall deal with a matter referred to it under this article only after it has ascertained that all domestic remedies have been invoked and exhausted in the matter, in conformity with the generally recognized principles of international law. This shall not be the rule where the application of the remedies is unreasonably prolonged or is unlikely to bring effective relief to the person who is the victim of the violation of this Convention;

(d) The Committee shall hold closed meetings when examining communications under this article;

(e) Subject to the provisions of subparagraph (c), the Committee shall make available its good offices to the States Parties concerned with a view to a friendly solution of the matter on the basis of respect for the obligations provided for in this Convention. For this purpose, the Committee may, when appropriate, set up an ad hoc conciliation commission;

(f) In any matter referred to it under this article, the Committee may call upon the States Parties concerned, referred to in subparagraph (b), to supply any relevant information;

(g) The States Parties concerned, referred to in subparagraph (b), shall have the right to be represented when the matter is being considered by the Committee and to make submissions orally and/or in writing;

(h) The Committee shall, within twelve months after the date of receipt of notice under subparagraph (b), submit a report:

(i) If a solution within the terms of subparagraph (e) is reached, the Committee shall confine its report to a brief statement of the facts and of the solution reached;

(ii) If a solution within the terms of suparagraph (e) is not reached, the Committee shall confine its report to a brief statement of the facts; the written submissions and record of the oral submissions made by the States Parties concerned shall be attached to the report.

In every matter, the report shall be communicated to the States Parties concerned.

2. The provisions of this article shall come into force when five States Parties to this Convention have made declarations under paragraph 1 of this article. Such declarations shall be deposited by the States Parties with the Secretary-General of the United Nations, who shall transmit copies thereof to the other States Parties. A declaration may be withdrawn at any time by notification to the Secretary-General. Such a withdrawal shall not prejudice the consideration of any matter which is the subject of a communication already transmitted under this article; no further communication by any State Party shall be received under this article after the notification of withdrawal of the declaration has been received by the Secretary-General, unless the State Party concerned has made a new declaration.

Article 22

1. A State Party to this Convention may at any time declare under this article that it recognizes the competence of the Committee to receive and consider communications from or on behalf of individuals subject to its jurisdiction who claim to be victims of a violation by a State Party of the provisions of the Convention. No communication shall be received by the Committee if it concerns a State Party which has not made such a declaration.

2. The Committee shall consider inadmissible any communication under this article which is anonymous or which it considers to be an abuse of the right of submission of such communications or to be incompatible with the provisions of the Convention.

3. Subject to the provisions of paragraph 2, the Committee shall bring any communications submitted to it under this article to the attention of the State Party of this Convention which has made a declaration under paragraph 1 and is alleged to be violating any provisions of the Convention. Within six months, the receiving State shall submit to the Committee written explanations or statements clarifying the matter and the remedy, if any, that may have been taken by that State.

4. The Committee shall consider communications received under this article in the light of all information made available to it by or on behalf of the individual and by the State Party concerned.

5. The Committee shall not consider any communications from an individual under this article unless it has ascertained that:

(a) The same matter has not been, and is not being, examined under another procedure of international investigation or settlement;

(b) The individual has exhausted all available domestic remedies; this shall not be the rule where the application of the remedies is unreasonably prolonged or is unlikely to bring effective relief to the person who is the victim of the violation of this Convention.

6. The Committee shall hold closed meetings when examining communications under this article.

7. The Committee shall forward its views to the State Party concerned and to the individual.

8. The provisions of this article shall come into force when five States Parties to this Convention have made declarations under paragraph 1 of this article. Such declarations shall be deposited by the States Parties with the Secretary-General of the United Nations, who shall transmit copies thereof to the other States Parties. A declaration may be withdrawn at any time by notification to the Secretary-General. Such a withdrawal shall not prejudice the consideration of any matter which is the subject of a communication already transmitted under this article; no further communication by or on behalf of an individual shall be received under this article after the notification of withdrawal of the declaration has been received by the Secretary-General, unless the State Party has made a new declaration.

Article 23

The members of the Committee and of the ad hoc conciliation commissions which may be appointed under article 21, paragraph 1(e), shall be entitled to the facilities, privileges and immunities of experts on mission for the United Nations as laid down in the relevant sections of the Convention on the Privileges and Immunities of the United Nations.

Article 24

The Committee shall submit an annual report on its activities under this Convention to the States Parties and to the Genearal Assembly of the United Nations.

PART III
Article 25

1. This Convention is open for signature by all States.

2. This Convention is subject to ratification. Instruments of ratification shall be deposited with the Secretary-General of the United Nations.

Article 26

This Convention is open to accession by all States. Accession shall be effected by the deposit of an instrument of accession with the Secretary-General of the United Nations.

Article 27

1. This Convention shall enter into force on the thirtieth day after the date of the deposit with the Secretary-General of the United Nations of the twentieth instrument of ratification or accession.

2. For each State ratifying this Convention or acceding to it after the deposit of the twentieth instrument of ratification or accession, the Convention shall enter into force on the thirtieth day after the date of the deposit of its own instrument of ratification or accession.

Article 28

1. Each State may, at the time of signature or ratification of this Convention

or accession thereto, declare that it does not recognize the competence of the Committee provided for in article 20.

2. Any State Party having made a reservation in accordance with paragraph 1 of this article may, at any time, withdraw this reservation by notification to the Secretary-General of the United Nations.

Article 29

1. Any State Party to this Convention may propose an amendment and file it with the Secretary-General of the United Nations. The Secretary-General shall thereupon communicate the proposed amendment to the States Parties with a request that they notify him whether they favour a conference of States Parties for the purpose of considering and voting upon the proposal. In the event that within four months from the date of such communication at least one third of the States Parties favours such a conference, the Secretary-General shall convene the conference under the auspices of the United Nations. Any amendment adopted by a majority of the States Parties present and voting at the conference shall be submitted by the Secretary-General to all the States Parties for acceptance.

2. An amendment adopted in accordance with paragraph 1 of this article shall enter into force when two thirds of the States Parties to this Convention have notified the Secretary-General of the United Nations that they have accepted it in accordance with their respective constitutional processes.

3. When amendments enter into force, they shall be binding on those States Parties which have accepted them, other States Parties still being bound by the provisions of this Convention and any earlier amendments which they have accepted.

Article 30

1. Any dispute between two or more States Parties concerning the interpretation or application of this Convention which cannot be settled through negotiation shall, at the request of one of them, be submitted to arbitration. If within six months from the date of the request for arbitration, any one of those Parties may refer the dispute to the International Court of Justice by request in conformity with the Statute of the Court.

2. Each State may, at the time of signature or ratification of this Convention or accession thereto, declare that it does not consider itself bound by paragraph 1 of this article. The other States Parties shall not be bound by paragraph 1 of this article with respect to any State Party having made such a reservation.

3. Any State Party having made a reservation in accordance with paragraph 2 of this article may at any time withdraw this reservation by notification to the Secretary-General of the United Nations.

Article 31

1. A State Party may denounce this Convention by written notification to the Secretary-General of the United Nations. Denunciation becomes effective one year after the date of receipt of the notification by the Secretary-General.

2. Such a denunciation shall not have the effect of releasing the State Party from its obligations under this Convention in regard to any act or omission which occurs prior to the date at which the denunciation becomes effective, nor shall denunciation prejudice in any way the continued consideration of any matter which is already under consideration by the Committee prior to the date at which the denunciation becomes effective.

3. Following the date at which the denunciation of a State Party becomes effective, the Committee shall not commence consideration of any new matter regarding that State.

Article 32

The Secretary-General of the United Nations shall inform all States Members of the United Nations and all States which have signed this Convention or acceded to it of the following:

(a) Signatures, ratifications and accessions under articles 25 and 26;

(b) The date of entry into force of this Convention under article 27 and the date of the entry into force of any amendments under article 29;

(c) Denunciations under article 31.

Article 33

1. This Convention, of which the Arabic, Chinese, English, French, Russian and Spanish texts are equally authentic, shall be deposited with the Secretary-General of the United Nations.

2. The Secretary-General of the United Nations shall transmit certified copies of this Convention to all States.

II Body of Principles for the Protection of All Persons under Any Form of Detention or Imprisonment

United Nations, 1988

Scope of the Body of Principles
These principles apply for the protection of all persons under any form of detention or imprisonment.

Use of Terms
For the purposes of the Body of Principles:

(a) 'Arrest' means the act of apprehending a person for the alleged commission of an offence or by the action of an authority;

(b) 'Detained' person means any person deprived of personal liberty as a result of conviction for an offence;

(d) 'Detention' means the condition of detained persons as defined above;

(e) 'Imprisonment' means the condition of imprisoned persons as defined above;

(f) The words 'a judicial or other authority' mean a judicial or other authority under the law whose status and tenure should afford the strongest possible guarantees of competence, impartiality and independence.

Principle 1
All persons under any form of detention or imprisonment shall be treated in a humane manner and with respect for the inherent dignity of the human person.

Principle 2
Arrest, detention or imprisonment shall only be carried out strictly in accordance with the provisions of the law and by competent officials or persons authorized for that purpose.

Principle 3
There shall be no restriction upon or derogation from any of the human rights of persons under any form of detention or imprisonment recognized or existing in any State pursuant to law, conventions, regulations or custom on the pretext that this Body of Principles does not recognize such rights or that it recognizes them to a lesser extent.

Principle 4
Any form of detention or imprisonment and all measures affecting the human rights of a person under any form of detention or imprisonment shall be ordered by, or be subject to the effective control of, a judicial or other authority.

Principle 5

1. These principles shall be applied to all persons within the territory of any given State, without distinction of any kind, such as race, colour, sex, language, religion or religious belief, political or other opinion, national, ethnic or social origin, property, birth or other status.

2. Measures applied under the law and designed solely to protect the rights and special status of women, especially pregnant women and nursing mothers, children and juveniles, aged, sick or handicapped persons, shall not be deemed to be discriminatory. The need for, and the application of, such measures shall always be subject to review by a judicial or other authority.

Principle 6

No person under any form of detention or imprisonment shall be subjected to torture or to cruel, inhuman or degrading treatment or punishment (the term 'cruel, inhuman or degrading treatment or punishment' should be interpreted so as to extend the widest possible protection against abuses, whether physical or mental, including the holding of a detained or imprisoned person in conditions which deprive him, temporarily or permanently, or the use of any of his natural senses, such as sight or hearing, or of his awareness of place and the passing of time). No circumstance whatever may be invoked as a justification for torture or other cruel, inhuman or degrading treatment or punishment.

Principle 7

1. States should prohibit by law any act contrary to the rights and duties contained in these principles, make any such act subject to appropriate sanctions and conduct impartial investigations upon complaints.

2. Officials who have reason to believe that a violation of this Body of Principles has occurred or is about to occur shall report the matter to their superior authorities and, where necessary, to other appropriate authorities or organs vested with reviewing or remedial powers.

3. Any other person who has ground to believe that a violation of this Body of Principles has occurred or is about to occur shall have the right to report the matter to the superiors of the officials involved as well as to other appropriate authorities or organs vested with reviewing or remedial powers.

Principle 8

Persons in detention shall be subject to treatment appropriate to their unconvicted status. Accordingly, they shall, whenever possible, be kept separate from imprisoned persons.

Principle 9

The authorities which arrest a person, keep him under detention or investigate the case shall exercise only the powers granted to them under the law and the exercise of these powers shall be subject to recourse to a judicial or other authority.

Principle 10

Anyone who is arrested shall be informed at the time of his arrest of the reason for his arrest and shall be promptly informed of any charges against him.

Principle 11

1. A person shall not be kept in detention without being given an effective opportunity to be heard promptly by a judicial or other authority. A detained person shall have the right to defend himself or to be assisted by counsel as prescribed by law.

2. A detained person and his counsel, if any, shall receive prompt and full communication of any order of detention, together with the reasons therefore.

3. A judicial or other authority shall be empowered to review as appropriate the continuance of detention.

Principle 12

1. There shall be duly recorded:

(a) The reasons for the arrest;

(b) The time of the arrest and the taking of the arrested person to a place of custody as well as that of his first appearance before a judicial or other authority;

(c) The identity of the law enforcement officials concerned;

(d) Precise information concerning the place of custody.

2. Such records shall be communicated to the detained person, or his counsel, if any, in the form prescribed by law.

Principle 13

Any person shall, at the moment of arrest and at the commencement of detention or imprisonment, or promptly thereafter, be provided by the authority responsible for his arrest, detention or imprisonment, respectively, with information on and an explanation of his rights and how to avail himself of such rights.

Principle 14

A person who does not adequately understand or speak the language used by the authorities responsible for his arrest, detention or imprisonment is entitled to receive promptly in a language which he understands the information referred to in principle 10, principle 11, paragraph 2, principle 12, paragraph 1, and principle 13 and to have the assistance, free of charge, if necessary, of an interpreter in connection with legal proceedings subsequent to his arrest.

Principle 15

Notwithstanding the exceptions contained in principle 16, paragraph 4, and principle 18, paragraph 3, communication of the detained or imprisoned person with the outside world, and in particular his family or counsel, shall not be denied for more than a matter of days.

Principle 16

1. Promptly after arrest and after each transfer from one place of detention or imprisonment to another, a detained or imprisoned person shall be entitled to notify or to require the competent authority to notify members of his family or other appropriate persons of his choice of his arrest, detention or imprisonment or of the transfer and of the place where he is kept in custody.

2. If a detained or imprisoned person is a foreigner, he shall also be promptly informed of his right to communicate by appropriate means with a consular post or the diplomatic mission of the State of which he is a national or which is otherwise entitled to receive such communication in accordance with international law or with the representative of the competent international organization, if he is a refugee or is otherwise under the protection of an intergovernmental organization.

3. If a detained or imprisoned person is a juvenile or is incapable of understanding his entitlement, the competent authority shall on its own initiative undertake the notification referred to in the present principle. Special attention shall be given to notifying parents or guardians.

4. Any notification referred to in the present principle shall be made or permitted to be made without delay. The competent authority may however delay a notification for a reasonable period where exceptional needs of the investigation so require.

Principle 17

1. A detained person shall be entitled to have the assistance of a legal counsel. He shall be informed of his right by the competent authority promptly after arrest and shall be provided with reasonable facilities for exercising it.

2. If a detained person does not have a legal counsel of his own choice, he shall be entitled to have a legal counsel assigned to him by a judicial or other authority in all cases where the interests of justice so require and without payment by him if he does not have sufficient means to pay.

Principle 18

1. A detained or imprisoned person shall be entitled to communicate and consult with his legal counsel.

2. A detained or imprisoned person shall be allowed adequate time and facilities for consultations with his legal counsel.

3. The right of a detained or imprisoned person to be visited by and to consult and communicate, without delay or censorship and in full confidentiality, with legal counsel may not be suspended or restricted save in exceptional circumstances, to be specified by law or lawful regulations, when it is considered indispensable by a judicial or other authority in order to maintain security and good order.

4. Interviews between a detained or imprisoned person and his legal counsel may be within sight, but not within the hearing, of a law enforcement official.

5. Communications between a detained or imprisoned person and his legal counsel mentioned in the present principle shall be inadmissible as evidence

against the detained or imprisoned person unless they are connected with a continuing or contemplated crime.

Principle 19

A detained or imprisoned person shall have the right to be visited by and to correspond with, in particular, members of his family and shall be given adequate opportunity to communicate with the outside world, subject to reasonable conditions and restrictions as specified by law or lawful regulations.

Principle 20

If detained or imprisoned person so requests, he shall if possible be kept in a place of detention or imprisonment reasonably near his usual place of residence.

Principle 21

1. It shall be prohibited to take undue advantage of the situation of a detained or imprisoned person for the purpose of compelling him to confess, to incriminate himself otherwise or to testify against any other person.

2. No detained person while being interrogated shall be subject to violence, threats or methods of interrogation which impair his capacity of decision or his judgement.

Principle 22

No detained or imprisoned person shall, even with his consent, be subjected to any medical or scientific experimentation which may be detrimental to his health.

Principle 23

1. The duration of any interrogation of a detained or imprisoned person and of the intervals between interrogations as well as the identity of the officials who conducted the interrogations and other persons present shall be recorded and certified in such form as may be prescribed by law.

2. A detained or imprisoned person, or his counsel when provided by law, shall have access to the information described in paragraph 1 of the present principle.

Principle 24

A proper medical examination shall be offered to a detained or imprisoned person as promptly as possible after his admission to the place of detention or imprisonment, and thereafter medical care and treatment shall be provided whenever necessary. This care and treatment shall be provided free of charge.

Principle 25

A detained or imprisoned person or his counsel shall, subject only to reasonable conditions to ensure security and good order in the place of detention or imprisonment, have the right to request or petition a judicial or other authority for a second medical examination or opinion.

Principle 26

The fact that a detained or imprisoned person underwent a medical examination, the name of the physician and the results of such an examination shall be duly recorded. Access to such records shall be ensured. Modalities therefore shall be in accordance with relevant rules of domestic law.

Principle 27

Non-compliance with these Principles in obtaining evidence shall be taken into account in determining the admissibility of such evidence against a detained or imprisoned person.

Principle 28

A detained or imprisoned person shall have the right to obtain within the limits of available resources, if from public sources, reasonable quantities of educational, cultural and informational material, subject to reasonable conditions to ensure security and good order in the place of detention or imprisonment.

Principle 29

1. In order to supervise the strict observance of relevant laws and regulations, places of detention shall be visited regularly by qualified and experienced persons appointed by, and responsible to, a competent authority distinct from the authority directly in charge of the administration of the place of detention or imprisonment.

2. A detained or imprisoned person shall have the right to communicate freely and in full confidentiality with the persons who visit the places of detention or imprisonment in accordance with paragraph 1 of the present principle, subject to reasonable conditions to ensure security and good order in such places.

Principle 30

The types of conduct of the detained or imprisoned person that constitute disciplinary offences during detention or imprisonment, the description and duration of disciplinary punishment that may be inflicted and the authorities competent to impose such punishment shall be specified by law or lawful regulations and duly published.

Principle 31

The appropriate authorities shall endeavour to ensure, according to domestic law, assistance when needed to dependent and, in particular, minor members of the families of detained or imprisoned persons and shall devote a particular measure of care to the appropriate custody of children left without supervision.

Principle 32

1. A detained person or his counsel shall be entitled at any time to take proceedings according to domestic law before a judicial or other authority to

challenge the lawfulness of his detention in order to obtain his release without delay, if it is unlawful.

2. The proceedings referred to in paragraph 1 of the present principle shall be simple and expeditious and at no cost for detained persons without adequate means. The detaining authority shall produce without unreasonable delay the detained person before the reviewing authority.

Principle 33

1. A detained or imprisoned person or his counsel shall have the right to make a request or complaint regarding his treatment, in particular in case of torture or other cruel, inhuman or degrading treatment, to the authorities responsible for the administration of the place of detention and to higher authorities and, when necessary, to appropriate authorities vested with reviewing or remedial powers.

2. In those cases where neither the detained or imprisoned person nor his counsel has the possibility to exercise his rights under paragraph 1 of the present principle, a member of the family of the detained or imprisoned person or any other person who has knowledge of the case may exercise such rights.

3. Confidentiality concerning the request or complaint shall be maintained if so requested by the complainant.

4. Every request or complaint shall be promptly dealt with and replied to without undue delay. If the request or complaint is rejected, or in case of inordinate delay, the complainant shall be entitled to bring it before a judicial or other authority. Neither the detained or imprisoned person nor any complainant under paragraph 1 of the present principle shall suffer prejudice for making a request or complaint.

Principle 34

Whenever the death or disappearance of a detained or imprisoned person occurs during his detention or imprisonment, an inquiry into the cause of death or disappearance shall be held by a judicial or other authority, either on its own motion or at the insistence of a member of the family of such a person or any person who has knowledge of the case. When circumstances so warrant, such an inquiry shall be held on the same procedural basis whenever the death or disappearance occurs shortly after the termination of the detention or imprisonment. The findings of such inquiry or a report thereon shall be made available upon request, unless doing so would jeopardize an ongoing criminal investigation.

Principle 35

1. Damage incurred because of acts or omissions by a public official contrary to the rights contained in these Principles shall be compensated according to the applicable rules on liability provided by domestic law.

2. Information required to be recorded under these Principles shall be available in accordance with procedures provided by domestic law for use in claiming compensation under the present principle.

154/TORTURE AND THE CASE OF ISRAEL

Principle 36

1. A detained person suspected of or charged with a criminal offence shall be presumed innocent and shall be treated as such until proved guilty according to law in a public trial at which he has had all the guarantees necessary for his defence.

2. The arrest or detention of such a person pending investigation and trial shall be carried out only for the purposes of the administration of justice on grounds and under conditions and procedures specified by law. The imposition of restrictions upon such a person which are not strictly required for the purpose of the detention or to prevent hindrance to the process of investigation or the administration of justice, or for the maintenance of security and good order in the place of detention, shall be forbidden.

Principle 37

A person detained on a criminal charge shall be brought before a judicial or other authority provided by law promptly after his arrest. Such authority shall decide without delay upon the lawfulness and necessity of detention. No person may be kept under detention pending investigation or trial except upon the written order of such an authority. A detained person shall, when brought before such an authority, have the right to make a statement on the treatment received by him while in custody.

Principle 38

A person detained on a criminal charge shall be entitled to trial within a reasonable time or to release pending trial.

Principle 39

Except in special cases provided for by law, a person detained on a criminal charge shall be entitled, unless a judicial or other authority decides otherwise in the interest of the administration of justice, to release pending trial subject to the conditions that may be imposed in accordance with the law. Such authority shall keep the necessity of detention under review.

General Clause

Nothing in this Body of Principles shall be construed as restricting or derogating from any right defined in the International Covenant on Civil and Political Rights.

Codes of medical ethics concerning torture

1 Hippocratic Oath

I swear by Apollo Physician and Asclepius and Hygieia and Panaceioa and all the gods and goddesses, making them my witnesses, that I will fulfil according to my ability and judgement this oath and this covenant:

To hold him who has taught me this art as equal to my parents and to live my life in partnership with him, and if he is in need of money to give him a share of mine, and to regard his offspring as equal to my brothers in male lineage and to teach them this art – if they desire to learn it – without fee and covenant; to give a share of precepts and oral instruction and all the other learning to my sons and to the sons of him who has instructed me and to pupils who have signed the covenant and have taken an oath according to the medical law, but to no one else.

I will apply dietetic measures for the benefit of the sick according to my ability and judgement; I will keep them from harm and injustice.

I will neither give a deadly drug to anybody if asked for it, nor will I make a suggestion to this effect. Similarly, I will not give to a woman an abortive remedy. In purity and holiness I will guard my life and my art.

I will not use the knife, not even on sufferers from stone, but will withdraw in favour of such men as are engaged in this work.

Whatever houses I may visit, I will come for the benefit of the sick, remaining free of all intentional injustice, of all mischief and in particular of sexual relations with both female and male persons, be they free or slaves.

What I may see or hear in the course of the treatment in regard to the life of men, which on no account one must spread abroad, I will keep to myself, holding such things shameful to be spoken about.

If I fulfil this oath and do not violate it, may it be granted to me to enjoy life and art, being honoured with fame among all men for all time to come; if I transgress it and swear falsely, may the opposite of all this be my lot.

II Prayer of Moses Maimonides

Moses Maimonides (1135–1204) was court physician to the sultan Saladin, the famous Muslim military leader. The prayer attributed to Maimonides is second only to the Hippocratic Oath in its influence on medical ethics. Excerpts are given below.

Almighty God, Thou hast created the human body with infinite wisdom ... Thou hast blest Thine earth, Thy rivers and Thy mountains with healing substances: they enable Thy creatures to alleviate their sufferings and to heal their illnesses. Thou hast endowed man with the wisdom to relieve the sufferings of his brother, to recognize his disorders, to extract the healing substances, to discover their powers and to prepare and to apply them to suit every ill. In Thine Eternal Providence, Thou hast chosen me to watch over the life and health of Thy creatures. I am now about to apply myself to the duties of my profession. Support me, Almighty God, in these great labours that they may benefit mankind, for without Thy help not even the least thing will succeed.

Inspire me with love for my Art and for Thy creatures. Do not allow thirst for profit, ambition for renown and admiration, to interfere with my profession, for these are the enemies of truth and of love for mankind and they can lead astray in the great task of attending to the welfare of Thy creatures. Preserve the strength of my body and of my soul that they ever be ready cheerfully to help and support rich and poor, good and bad, enemy as well as friend. In the sufferer let me see only the human being. Illumine my mind that it may recognize what presents itself and that it may comprehend what is absent or hidden ...

Should those who are wiser than I wish to improve and instruct me, let my soul gratefully follow their guidance ...

Imbue my soul with gentleness and calmness ...

Let me be contented in everything except the great science of my profession. Never allow the thought to arise in me that I have attained to sufficient knowledge, but vouchsafe to me the strength, the leisure and the ambition ever to extend my knowledge. For Art is great, but the mind of man is ever expanding.

Almighty God! Thou has chosen me in Thy mercy to watch over the life and death of Thy creatures. I now apply myself to my profession. Support me in this great task so that it may benefit mankind, for without Thy help not even the least thing will succeed.

III Declaration of Tokyo

The Declaration of Tokyo has been, since its adoption in 1975 by the World Medical Association, the most comprehensive statement produced by the medical profession on the question of torture and cruel, inhuman or degrading treatment of detainees. It was adopted by the Twenty-Ninth World Medical Assembly, Tokyo, Japan. The text is as follows.

It is the privilege of the medical doctor to practise medicine in the service of humanity, to preserve and restore bodily and mental health without distinction as to persons, to comfort and to ease the suffering of his or her patients. The utmost respect for human life is to be maintained even under threat, and no use made of any medical knowledge contrary to the laws of humanity.

For the purpose of this Declaration, torture is defined as the deliberate, systematic or wanton infliction of physical or mental suffering by one or more persons acting alone or on the orders of any authority, to force another person to yield information, to make a confession, or for any other reason.

1. The doctor shall not countenance, condone or participate in the practice of torture or other forms of cruel, inhuman or degrading procedures, whatever the offence of which the victim of such procedures is suspected, accused or guilty, and whatever the victim's beliefs or motives, and in all situations, including armed conflict and civil strife.

2. The doctor shall not provide any premises, instruments, substances or knowledge to facilitate the practice of torture or other forms of cruel, inhuman or degrading treatment or to diminish the ability of the victim to resist such treatment.

3. The doctor shall not be present during any procedure during which torture or other forms of cruel, inhuman or degrading treatment is used or threatened.

4. A doctor must have complete clinical independence in deciding upon the care of a person for whom he or she is medically responsible. The doctor's fundamental role is to alleviate the distress of his or her fellow men, and no motive, whether personal, collective or political, shall prevail against this higher purpose.

5. Where a prisoner refuses nourishment and is considered by the doctor as capable of forming an unimpaired and rational judgement concerning the consequences of such a voluntary refusal of nourishment, he or she shall not be fed artificially. The decision as to the capacity of the prisoner to form such a judgement should be confirmed by at least one other independent doctor. The consequences of the refusal of nourishment shall be explained by the doctor to the prisoner.

6. The World Medical Association will support, and should encourage the international community, the national medical associations and fellow doctors to support, the doctor and his or her family in the face of threats or reprisals resulting from a refusal to condone the use of torture or other forms of cruel, inhuman or degrading treatment.

Principles of medical ethics

The Principles are elaborated within the text of the Resolution 37/194, adopted by the United Nations General Assembly on 18 December 1982: 'Principles of medical ethics relevant to the role of health personnel, particularly physicians, in the protection of prisoners and detainees against torture and other cruel, inhuman or degrading treatment or punishment'.

The General Assembly ...

Desirous of setting further standards in this field which ought to be implemented by health personnel, particularly physicians, and by government officials,

1. Adopts the Principles of Medical Ethics relevant to the role of health personnel, particularly physicians, in the protection of prisoners and detainees against torture and other cruel, inhuman or degrading treatment or punishment set forth in the annex to the present resolution;

2. Calls upon all Governments to give the Principles of Medical Ethics, together with the present resolution, the widest possible distribution, in particular among medical and paramedical associations and institutions of detention or imprisonment in an official language of the state.

3. Invites all relevant inter-governmental organizations, in particular the World Health Organization, and non-governmental organizations concerned to bring the Principles of Medical Ethics to the attention of the widest possible group of individuals, especially those active in the medical and paramedical field.

Principles of medical ethics relevant to the role of health personnel, particularly physicians, in the protection of prisoners and detainees against torture and other cruel, inhuman or degrading treatment or punishment

Principle 1

Health personnel, particularly physicians, charged with the medical care of prisoners and detainees have the duty to provide them with protection of their physical and mental health and treatment of disease of the same quality and standard as is afforded to those who are not imprisoned or detained.

Principle 2

It is a gross contravention of medical ethics, as well as an offence under applicable international instruments, for health personnel, particularly physicians, to engage, actively or passively, in acts which constitute participation in, complicity in, incitement to or attempts to commit torture or other cruel, inhuman or degrading treatment or punishment.

Principle 3

It is a contravention of medical ethics for health personnel, particularly physicians, to be involved in any professional relationship with prisoners or detainees the purpose of which is not to solely evaluate, protect or improve their physical and mental health.

Principle 4

It is a contravention of medical ethics for health personnel, particularly physicians:

a) To apply their knowledge and skills in order to assist in the interrogation of prisoners and detainees in a manner that may adversely affect the physical or mental health of such prisoners or detainees and which is not in accordance with the relevant international instruments.

b) To certify, or to participate in the certification of, the fitness of prisoners or detainees for any form of treatment or punishment that may adversely affect their physical or mental health and which is not in accordance with the relevant international instruments, or to participate in any way in the infliction of any such treatment or punishment which is not in accordance with the relevant international instruments.

Principle 5

It is a contravention of medical ethics for health personnel, particularly physicians, to participate in any procedure for restraining a prisoner or detainee unless such a procedure is determined in accordance with purely medical criteria as being necessary for the protection of the physical or mental health or the safety of the prisoner or detainee himself, of his fellow prisoners or detainees, or of his guardians, and presents no hazard to his physical or mental health.

Principle 6

There may be no derogation from the foregoing principles on any grounds whatsoever, including public emergency.

v International Code of Medical Ethics

One of the first acts of the World Medical Association, when formed in 1947, was to produce a modern restatement of the Hippocratic Oath, known as the Declaration of Geneva, and to base upon it an International Code of Medical Ethics which applies in time of both peace and war. The Declaration of Geneva, as amended by the Twenty-Second World Medical Assembly, Sydney, Australia, in August 1968, and the Thirty-Fifth World Medical Assembly, Venice, Italy, in October 1983, reads:

At the time of being admitted as a member of the Medical Profession:

I solemnly pledge myself to consecrate my life to the service of humanity;

I will give to my teachers the respect and gratitude which is their due;

I will practise my profession with conscience and dignity;

The health of my patient will be my first consideration;

I will respect the secrets which are confided in me, even after the patient has died;

I will maintain by all the means in my power, the honour and the noble traditions of the medical profession;

My colleagues will be my brothers;

I will not permit considerations of religion, nationality, race, party politics or social standing to intervene between my duty and my patients;

I will maintain the utmost respect for human life from its beginning even under threat and I will not use my medical knowledge contrary to the laws of humanity;

I make these promises solemnly, freely and upon my honour.

The English text of the International Code of Medical Ethics is as follows.

Duties of physicians in general

A physician shall always maintain the highest standards of professional conduct.

A physician shall not permit motives of profit to influence the free and independent exercise of professional judgement on behalf of patients.

A physician shall, in all types of medical practice, be dedicated to providing competent medical service in full technical and moral independence, with compassion and respect for human dignity.

A physician shall deal honestly with patients and colleagues, and strive to expose those physicians deficient in character or competence, or who engage in fraud or deception.

The following practices are deemed to be unethical conduct:

(a) Self-advertising by physicians, unless permitted by the laws of the country and the Code of Ethics of the national medical association.

(b) Paying or receiving any fee or any other consideration solely to procure the referral of a patient or for prescribing or referring a patient to any source.

A physician shall respect the rights of patients, of colleagues, and of other health professionals, and shall safeguard patient confidences.

A physician shall act only in the patient's interest when providing medical care which might have the effect of weakening the physical and mental condition of the patient.

A physician shall use great caution in divulging discoveries or new techniques or treatment through non-professional channels.

A physician shall certify only that which he has personally verified.

Duties of physicians to the sick

A physician shall always bear in mind the obligation of preserving human life.

A physician shall owe his patients complete loyalty and all the resources of his science. Whenever an examination or treatment is beyond the physician's capacity he should summon another physician who has the necessary ability.

A physician shall preserve absolute confidentiality on all he knows about his patient even after the patient has died.

A physician shall give emergency care as a humanitarian duty unless he is assured that others are willing and able to give such care.

Duties of physicians to each other

A physician shall behave towards his colleagues as he would have them behave towards him.

A physician shall not entice patients from his colleagues.

A physician shall observe the principles of 'The Declaration of Geneva' approved by the World Medical Association.

Subsequently, the World Medical Association has considered and published material on a number of ethical matters.

VI Ethical principles relative to the medical care of detainees

Incorporated into the Ethical Code of the Chilean Medical Association on 7 May 1985. Complements Article 25 of the said Code.

1. The doctor may never attend any person under the following conditions:
1.1 If the doctor is prevented from identifying himself.
1.2 If the doctor is covered or hooded, or his identity is in any other way concealed.
1.3 If the patient is blindfolded (for non-medical reasons) or in any other way prevented from seeing the doctor.
1.4 In any place of detention other than his home or a publicly recognized place of detention.
1.5 In the presence of third parties who impede free contact or alter the normal relationship between doctor and patient.
2. The doctor must identify himself if the patient asks it. Under no circumstances may he refuse such a request.
3. No doctor may participate, even as an observer, in sessions of interrogation, nor may he ever inform the interrogators or other related people of the physical or mental capacity of the person under interrogation to withstand illegal pressure. Furthermore, he may not establish any professional relationship with the detainee which does not have, as its sole purpose, the benefit of the patient.
4. Doctors who are required to examine or otherwise attend detainees must in additon to adhering to the above rules, identify themselves fully with their complete name, Association number, and identity card number in all certificates and documents they issue and in clear and legible writing.
5. The doctor must carry out medical examinations only when he has the freedom necessary to perform the examination, make a diagnosis and note his findings.
6. If, for reasons of strict medical emergency, or under threat, pressure or compulsion, a doctor is prevented from wholly fulfilling the above obligations, he should, within a maximum of 5 working days, inform the Regional Council of this who will investigate his complaint. The Medical Association will treat this information in the strictest confidence if the complainant so requires.

VII   Statement of Madrid

'Recommendations Concerning Doctors, Ethics, and Torture', Madrid, Spain, November 1989.

Having taken into consideration the recommendations of the international meeting on Doctors, Ethics, and Torture held in Copenhagen on 23 August 1986, the Plenary Assembly of the Standing Committee of Doctors of the European Communities, meeting in Madrid on 24–25 November 1989, deliberated the problems faced by doctors and the organized medical profession in countries where torture is or has been employed.

The Plenary Assembly of the Standing Committee of Doctors of the EC agreed:

— to urge all national medical associations which have not yet done so to ratify, publicise, and implement the Declaration of Tokyo (Guidelines for Medical Doctors Concerning Torture and Other Cruel, Inhuman or Degrading Treatment or Punishment in Relation to Detention and Imprisonment) adopted by the World Medical Association in 1975 as the definitive statement of the position of the medical profession on this topic;

— to urge the inclusion and integration in the medical educational curricula of information about the existence of this problem and instruction in the ethical responsibilities and regulations by which the doctor is bound and to which he may refer when subjected to pressure to act contrary to the best ethical principles of the medical profession;

— to urge all national governments which have not yet done so to ratify and implement the United Nations Declaration of 1982 and other relevant international declarations on this topic;

— to urge all scientific and professional medical bodies and the profession in all countries to incorporate the principles of the Tokyo Declaration into their statutes, and all other relevant documents, including a principle stating that a doctor shall never participate – directly or indirectly and even by his own presence – in a process or accept a procedure of any nature assigned to violate the physical or mental integrity of a person or the human dignity;

— to urge the establishment of an international reporting system regarding ethical infractions within the profession in this respect and to publicise information about the existence of torture and to urge that similar educational measures be taken for all health professions and police and military personnel, and to encourage and support research against torture and for treatment of the victims of torture; and

— to urge that international support be given to colleagues who take action to resist the involvement of doctors in such procedures and to mount an international protest against any efforts to hinder the profession in attempts to uphold the highest ethical principles of physicians.

VIII Declaration of Hawaii

World Psychiatric Association, 1977, revised 1983.

Ever since the dawn of culture, ethics has been an essential part of the healing art. It is the view of the World Psychiatric Association that due to conflicting loyalties and expectations of both physicians and patients in contemporary society, and the delicate nature of the therapist–patient relationship, high ethical standards are especially important for those involved in the science and practice of psychiatry as a medical speciality. These guidelines have been delineated in order to promote close adherence to those standards and to prevent misuse of psychiatric concepts, knowledge and technology.

Since the psychiatrist is a member of society as well as a practitioner of medicine, he or she must consider the ethical implications specific to psychiatry as well as the ethical demands on all physicians and the societal responsibility of every man and woman.

Even though ethical behavior is based on the individual psychiatrist's conscience and personal judgement, written guidelines are needed to clarify the profession's ethical implications.

Therefore, the General Assembly of the World Psychiatric Association has approved the following ethical guidelines for psychiatrists, having in mind the great differences in cultural backgrounds and in legal, social and economic conditions which exist in the various countries of the world. It should be understood that the World Psychiatric Association views these guidelines to be minimal requirements for ethical standards of the psychiatric profession.

1. The aim of psychiatry is to treat mental illness and to promote mental health. To the best of his or her ability, consistent with accepted scientific and ethical principles, the psychiatrist shall serve the best interest of the patient and be also concerned for the common good and a just allocation of health resources. To fulfill these aims requires continuous research and continual education of health care personnel, patients and the public.

2. Every psychiatrist should offer to the patient the best therapy available to his knowledge and if accepted must treat him or her with the solicitude and respect due to all human beings. When the psychiatrist is responsible for treatment given by others he owes them competent supervision and education. Whenever there is a need, or whenever a reasonable request is forthcoming from the patient, the psychiatrist should seek the help of another colleague.

3. A psychiatrist aspires for a therapeutic relationship that is founded on mutual agreement. Such a relationship requires confidentiality, cooperation and mutual responsibility. Such a relationship may not be possible to establish with some patients. In that case, contact should be established with a relative or other person close to the patient. If and when a relationship is established for purposes other than therapeutic, such as in forensic psychiatry, its nature must be thoroughly explained to the person concerned.

4. The psychiatrist should inform the patient of the nature of the condition, of therapeutic procedures, including possible alternatives, and of the possible outcome. This information must be offered in a considerate way and the patient be given the opportunity to choose between appropriate and available methods.

5. No procedure shall be performed or treatment given against or independent of a patient's own will, unless because of mental illness, the patient cannot form a judgement as to what is in his or her own best interest and without which treatment serious impairment is likely to occur to the patient or others.

6. As soon as the conditions for compulsory treatment no longer apply, the psychiatrist should release the patient from the compulsory nature of the treatment and if further therapy is necessary should obtain voluntary consent. The psychiatrist should inform the patient, and/or relatives or meaningful others, of the existence of mechanisms of appeal of the detention and for any other complaints related to his or her well-being.

7. The psychiatrist must never use his professional possibilities to violate the dignity or human rights of any individual or group and should never let inappropriate personal desires, feelings, prejudices or beliefs interfere with the treatment. The psychiatrist must on no account utilize the tools of his profession, once the absence of psychiatric illness has been established. If a patient or some third party demands actions contrary to scientific knowledge or ethical principles the psychiatrist must refuse to cooperate.

8. Whatever the psychiatrist has been told by the patient, or has noted during examination or treatment, must be kept confidential unless the patient relieves the psychiatrist from this obligation, or to prevent serious harm to self or others makes disclosure necessary. In these cases, however, the patient should be informed of the breach of confidentiality.

9. To increase and propagate psychiatric knowledge and skill requires participation of the patients. Informed consent must, however, be obtained before presenting a patient to a class, and if possible, also when a case history is released for scientific publication, whereby all reasonable measures must be taken to preserve the dignity and anonymity of the patient and to safeguard the personal reputation of the subject. The patient's participation must be voluntary, after full information has been given of the aim, procedures, risks and inconveniences of a research project and there must always be reasonable relationship between calculated risks or inconveniences and the benefit of the study. In clinical research every subject must retain and exert all his rights as a patient. For children and other patients who cannot themselves give informed consent, this should be obtained from the legal next-of-kin. Every patient or research subject is free to withdraw for any reason at any time from any voluntary treatment and from any teaching or research program in which he or she participates. This withdrawal, as well as any refusal to enter a program, must never influence the psychiatrist's efforts to help the patient or subject.

10. The psychiatrist should stop all therapeutic, teaching or research programs that may evolve contrary to the principles of this Declaration.

IX Statement on the role of the nurse in the care of detainees and prisoners

At the meeting of the Council of National Representatives of the International Council of Nurses (ICN) in Singapore in August 1975, the following statement was adopted.

WHEREAS the ICN Code for Nurses specifically states that:

1. The fundamental responsibility of the nurse is fourfold: to promote health, to prevent illness, to restore health and to alleviate suffering.

2. The nurse's primary responsibility is to those people who require nursing care.

3. The nurse when acting in a professional capacity should at all times maintain standards of personal conduct which reflect credit upon the profession.

4. The nurse takes appropriate action to safeguard the individual when his care is endangered by a co-worker or any other person; and

WHEREAS in 1973 ICN reaffirmed support for the Red Cross Rights and Duties of Nurses under the Geneva Conventions of 1949, which specifically state that, in case of armed conflict of international as well as national character (i.e. internal disorders, civil wars, armed rebellions):

1. Members of the armed forces, prisoners and persons taking no active part in the hostilities

(a) shall be entitled to protection and care if wounded or sick,

(b) shall be treated humanely, that is:

— they may not be subjected to physical mutilation or to medical or scientific experiments of any kind which are not justified by the medical, dental or hospital treatment of the prisoner concerned and carried out in his interest,

— they shall not be wilfully left without medical assistance and care, nor shall conditions exposing them to contagion or infection be created,

— they shall be treated humanely and cared for by the Party in conflict in whose power they may be, without adverse distinction founded on sex, race, nationality, religion, political opinion, or any other similar criteria.

2. The following acts are and shall remain prohibited at any time and in any place whatsoever with respect to the above-mentioned persons:

(a) violence to life and person, in particular murder of all kinds, mutilation, cruel treatment and torture;

(b) outrages upon personal dignity, in particular humiliating and degrading treatment; and

WHEREAS in 1971 ICN endorsed the United Nations Universal Declaration of Human Rights and, hence, accepted that:

1. Everyone is entitled to all the rights and freedoms, set forth in this

Declaration, without distinction of any kind, such as race, colour, sex, language, religion, political or other opinion, national or social origin, property, birth or other status (Art. 2).

2. No one shall be subjected to torture or to cruel, inhuman or degrading treatment or punishment (Art. 5); and

WHEREAS in relation to detainees and prisoners of conscience interrogation procedures are increasingly being employed which result in ill-effects, often permanent, on the person's mental and physical health;

THEREFORE BE IT RESOLVED that ICN condemns the use of all such procedures harmful to the mental and physical health of prisoners and detainees; and

FURTHER BE IT RESOLVED that nurses having knowledge of physical or mental ill-treatment of detainees and prisoners take appropriate action including reporting the matter to appropriate national and or international bodies; and

FURTHER BE IT RESOLVED that nurses participate in clinical research carried out on prisoners, only if the freely given consent of the patient has been secured after a complete explanation and understanding by the patient of the nature and risk of the research; and

FINALLY BE IT RESOLVED that the nurse's first responsibility is towards her patients, notwithstanding considerations of national security and interest.

x Statement on the nurse's role in safeguarding human rights

Responding to requests from national member associations for guidance on the protection of human rights of both nurses and those for whom they care, the Council of National Representatives of the International Council of Nurses (ICN) adopted the statement given below at its meeting in Brasilia, Brazil, in June 1983.

This document has been developed in response to the requests of national nurses' associations for guidance in assisting nurses to safeguard their own human rights and those for whom they have professional responsibility. It is meant to be used in conjunction with the ICN Code for Nurses and resolutions relevant to human rights. Nurses should also be familiar with the Geneva Conventions and the additional protocols as they relate to the responsibilities of nurses.

The current world situation is such that there are innumerable circumstances in which a nurse may become involved that require action on her/his part to safeguard human rights. Nurses are accountable for their own professional actions and must therefore be clear as to what is expected of them in such situations.

Also conflict situations have increased in number and often include internal political upheaval, and strife, or international war. The nature of war is changing. Increasingly nurses find themselves having to act or respond in complex situations to which there seems to be no clear-cut solution.

Changes in the field of communications also have increased the awareness and sensitivity of all groups to those conflict situations.

The need for nursing actions to safeguard human rights is not restricted to times of political upheaval and war. It can also arise in prisons or in the normal work situation of any nurse where abuse of patients, nurses, or others is witnessed or suspected. Nurses have a responsibility in each of these situations to take action to safeguard the rights of those involved. Physical abuse and mental abuse are equally of concern to the nurse. Over- or under-treatment is another area to be watched. There may be pressures applied to use one's knowledge and skills in ways that are not beneficial to patients or others.

Scientific discoveries have brought about more sophisticated forms of torture and methods of resuscitation so that those being tortured can be kept alive for repeated sessions. It is in such circumstances that nurses must be clear about what actions they must take as in no way can they participate in such torture, or torture techniques.

Nurses have individual responsibility but often they can be more effective if they approach human rights issues as a group. The national nurses' associations need to ensure that their structure provides a realistic mechanism through which nurses can seek confidential advice, counsel, support and assistance in dealing with these difficult situations. Verification of the facts reported will be an important first step in any particular situation.

At times it will be appropriate for the NNA [National Nurses' Association] to become a spokesman for the nurses involved. They may also be required to negotiate for them. It is essential that confidentiality be maintained. In rare cases the personal judgment of the nurse may be such that other actions seem more appropriate than approaching the Association.

The nurse initiating the actions requires knowledge of her own and others' human rights, moral courage, a well thought through plan of action and a commitment and determination to see that the necessary follow-up does occur. Personal risk is a factor that has to be considered and each person must use her/his best judgment in the situation.

Rights of those in need of care

— Health care is a right of all individuals. Everyone should have access to health care regardless of financial, political, geographic, racial or religious considerations. The nurse should seek to ensure such impartial treatment.
— Nurses must ensure that adequate treatment is provided – within available resources – and in accord with nursing ethics (ICN Code) to all those in need of care.
— A patient/prisoner has the right to refuse to eat or to refuse treatments. The nurse may need to verify that the patient/prisoner understands the implications of such action but she should not participate in the administration of food or medications to such patients.

Rights and duties of nurses

— When considering the rights and duties of nursing personnel it needs to be remembered that both action and lack of action can have a detrimental effect and the nursing personnel must be considered accountable on both counts.
— Nurses have a right to practise within the code of ethics and nursing legislation of the country in which they practise. Personal safety – freedom from abuse, threats or intimidation – is the right of every nurse.
— National nurses' associations have a responsibility to participate in development of health and social legislation relative to patients' rights and all related topics.
— It is a duty to have informed consent of patients relative to having research done on them and in receiving treatments such as blood transfusions, anaesthesia, grafts etc. Such informed consent is a patient's right and must be ensured.

XI Statement on nurses and torture

The statement on nurses and torture was adopted at the meeting of the Council of National Representatives of the International Council of Nurses in Seoul, South Korea, in May 1989. The text, last reviewed in 1991, is given below.

Violations of human rights have become more pervasive and scientific discoveries have brought about more sophisticated forms of torture and methods of resuscitation.

Although nurses may not voluntarily participate in any form of physical or psychological torture, they must know what is expected of them and what action they must take to safeguard human rights.

Nurses need to know that, although the apparent motive for much of the treatment during and after torture is the protection of the victim, it is often carried out more as protection of the torturers. The nurse may be called upon to act alone or to assist in the following situations:

— to perform physical examinations on suspects before they are subjected to forms of interrogation, which might include torture
— to attend a torture session in order to intervene when the victim's life is in danger
— to treat the direct physical effects of torture, so that later the interrogation can be continued.

The nurse's primary responsibility is to those people who require nursing care. If the victim of cruel, wanton, degrading or any other inhuman procedure or treatment (in the independent opinion of the nurse) requires nursing care, then no motive should prevail against the nurse giving such care to the highest standard possible.

The national nurses' associations (NNA) need to ensure that their structure provides a realistic mechanism through which nurses can seek confidential advice, counsel, support and assistance in dealing with these difficult situations. Verification of the facts reported will be an important first step in any particular case.

The responsiblity of the nurse

The nurse shall not countenance, condone or voluntarily participate in:

— any deliberate, systematic or wanton infliction of physical or mental suffering or any other form of cruel, inhuman or degrading procedure by one or more persons acting alone or on the orders of any authority, to force another person to yield information, to make a confession or for any other reason
— any treatment which denies to any person the respect which is his/her due as a human being.

Documents concerning practice of torture in Israel

1 Proposed bill for the prohibition of torture as an amendment to Israeli penal law (1992)

Foreword

The government has recently decided to ratify the international covenant whose title is 'Covenant Against Torture and Other Cruel, Inhuman or Degrading Treatment or Punishment'.

Under Clause 2 of the convention the government of Israel commits itself to using legislative and other means to prevent abuse. The above bill is intended to incorporate into Israeli law the clauses in the convention concerning the obligations of states that are signatories to the convention thus providing these clauses with legal authority.

The clauses of the international convention which are relevant to the proposed bill are:

Part 1, Article 1

For the purposes of this Convention, the term 'torture' means any act by which severe pain or suffering, whether physical or mental, is intentionally inflicted on a person for such purposes as obtaining from him or a third person information or a confession, punishing him for an act he or a third person has committed or is suspected of having committed, or intimidating or coercing him or a third person, or for any reason based on discrimination of any kind, when such pain or suffering is inflicted by or at the instigation of or with the consent or acquiescence of a public official or other person acting in an official capacity. It does not include pain or suffering arising only from, inherent in or incidental to lawful sanctions.

Article 5

Each State Party shall take such measures as may be necessary to establish its jurisdiction over the offences referred to in article 4 in the following cases:

a. When the offences are committed in any territory under its jurisdiction or on board a ship or aircraft registered in that State;

b. When the alleged offender is a national of that State;

c. When the victim is a national of that State if that State considers it appropriate.

Article 15

Each State Party shall ensure that any statement which is established to have been made as a result of torture shall not be invoked as evidence in any proceedings, except against a person accused of torture as evidence that the statement was made.

1. To be added to Section 10 of the Penal Law
Article 9 Prohibition of torture

382A

A. For the purposes of this Article, torture is an act carried out by a public official or other person acting in an official capacity, or with his consent, or at his instigation, or with his acquiescence and by means of which pain or severe suffering is caused to a person intentionally, this being:

1. With the intent of obtaining information or a confession from him or a third person, of punishing him for an act he or a third person has committed or is suspected of having committed, or in order to intimidate or coerce him or a third person.

2. Or for any reason stemming from discrimination of any kind whatsoever.

B. Pain or suffering for the purposes of this clause do not include pain or suffering arising from legal sanctions, inherent in or incidental to them.

382B

A. A person convicted of torture shall be sentenced to seven years imprisonment and no less than one year.

B. A person convicted of torture causing serious damage shall be sentenced to twenty years imprisonment.

C. A person convicted of torture causing death shall be sentenced to life imprisonment and no other penalty.

D. A public employee who has knowledge that a torture offence has been committed and has not used all reasonable means to prevent or cease the torture, shall be sentenced to the same sentence as the offender.

382C

The defences in clauses 22, 23, 24 of this law shall not apply to a person committing an offence under this item.

2. To be added to the Penal Law

7.B Israeli courts shall have jurisdiction over an Israeli citizen or resident of Israel who has committed an offence under Article 9 of this law abroad.

3. To be added to the Orders on Evidence (new version)

12.A Information acquired as a result of the use of torture within its meaning under the penal law, will be inadmissible as evidence in court, with the exception of proceedings against a person accused or sued for use of torture or for failure to prevent it.

The above proposed bill is presented after consultation with the Association for Civil Rights in Israel.

Proposed by:

MK [Member of Knesset] *Tamar Gojanski*
MK Haim Oron
MK Tufiq Ziad
MK Avraham Poraz
MK Hashem Mahmid

MK Shlomo Benizri
MK Yael Dayan
MK Nawaf Masalcha
MK Naomi Chazan

11 Letter to the Minister of Justice

Letter written by Eliahu Abram, the Association of Civil Rights in Israel, to the Minister of Justice in Israel.

Regarding: Proposed Bill Against Torture

On the 16th of June, 1993, Members of Knesset from various parties will bring before the Knesset for an initial vote a bill against torture. The bill is identical to the text proposed in the previous session of the Knesset – Penal Law (Amendment – Prohibition of Torture) 1992.

We request that you consider supporting the initial proposal in order that it can be referred to the Knesset Constitution Law and Justice Committee for deliberation. The proposed bill deserves consideration by the Committee as a basis for legislation on the issue.

In our opinion, ratification of the Convention against Torture and Other Cruel, Inhuman or Degrading Treatment or Punishment requires internal legislation. According to section 4(1) of the Convention: 'Each State Party shall ensure that all acts of torture are offences under its criminal law ... '

In addition, States must ensure that the punishment for crimes of torture gives appropriate expression to the severity of the offence (section 4(2)), that courts are granted universal jurisdiction over offences of torture and that these offences be extraditable (sections 5, 7 and 8). Furthermore, the inadmissibility in evidence of statements taken as a result of torture must be assured (section 15).

Many countries have already adopted specific legislation on this matter pursuant to their ratification of the Convention. These countries recognized a need to establish a new offence in accordance with the definition of 'torture' under section 1 of the Convention, despite the existence of general offences in their penal laws which prohibit the use or force, threats or extortion.

I attach herein for your examination the laws enacted on this issue in England, Canada, New Zealand, the Netherlands and Mexico. Rumania and Greece also have specific legislation governing the topic, and I enclose the relevant sections of their reports to the U.N. Committee against Torture. Other countries, including France, reported to the U.N. Committee that legislation was under consideration.

The English law applies to the entire United Kingdom, including Northern Ireland, where terror is a continuing problem. Britain was accused in the past of using methods of interrogation in Northern Ireland which amount to torture – an accusation raised in the European Court of Human Rights. This fact did not deter the British government from initiating legislation against torture. According to sections 134 through 138 of the Criminal Justice Act, 1988, the prohibition of torture includes causing severe mental suffering, by act or omission, without force or threats being a necessary element of the offence.

Jurisdiction of the British courts over the offence is universal and the crime of torture is made an extraditable felony. The maximum penalty is life imprisonment, as is fitting for a crime against confessions obtained by means of torture was already included in section 76(8) of Police and Criminal Evidence Act of 1984, adopted pursuant to the prohibition against torture in section 3 of the European Convention of Human Rights (see Cross on Evidence, 6th ed., p. 549).

I have dwelt on the British law only because of the known connection between British and Israeli criminal law, extradition law and law of evidence, and in view of our common principles concerning the incorporation of international treaties in internal legislation. The other states mentioned above also enacted laws which are both comprehensive and impressive.

In our opinion, it cannot be seriously argued that Israeli law meets the terms of the Convention in full.

Causing mental suffering without the use of force or threats or the infliction of bodily injury is not currently prohibited under our Penal Law, with the exception of 'cruel treatment of a minor or a helpless person' under section 368(c) of the Law. There can be no doubt that this section, as well as the entire chapter of the Law in which it appears, was not intended to apply to a person under interrogation: an interrogee is unlikely to fit the definition of 'helpless person', and the duty to report a suspected act of abuse to the police or welfare officer is inappropriate to the situation of interrogation conducted by the police itself or by another public employee. Causing severe mental suffering without bodily injury is a sign of the sophistication of torture in our times.

The offences under section 277 of the Penal Law, 'pressure by a public official', is the closest and the most specific to the subject matter of the Convention. This offence is a misdemeanor.

The penalty of three years imprisonment does not express the gravity of a crime against humanity. There is no provision in Chapter Two of the Penal Law extending universal jurisdiction over offences of torture – and it would be inconceivable to extend universal jurisdiction over the existing general offences.

A statement taken by means of torture may be admissible under section 10A of the Evidence Ordinance (concerning the admissibility of out-of-court statements of witnesses).

There is also great declarative value in establishing a specific crime against torture.

The State of Israel, having joined the Convention against Torture, should also join those enlightened states who take their obligations under this Convention seriously. Specific legislation implementing the Convention would bring credit to the State of Israel, and would not be self-accusatory. On the contrary, refraining from legislating on this topic would present our country in a negative light, as if we had something to fear from a total and severe prohibition of torture.

The previous Government already determined that we have nothing to fear from the terms of the Convention against Torture. On the present Government – in which you represent the values of our legal system – falls the duty to cooperate with the Knesset in framing the legislation required to implement the Convention's provisions.

III Letter presented by the Conference on the International Struggle against Torture and the Case of Israel

The following letter was distributed before the Conference on the International Struggle against Torture and the Case of Israel and was signed by approximately 4,000 organizations and individuals. The signatures were later presented to the Israeli Justice Minister at a meeting headed by Dr Ruchama Marton, Chairperson of the Association of Israeli–Palestinian Physicians for Human Rights.

We, the undersigned, call on the State of Israel to establish clearly and unambiguously that it in no way condones the practice of torture; that it is committed to the thorough investigation of allegations of torture and to the prosecution of alleged torturers. We call upon the Minister of Justice and the Knesset of Israel to undertake express legislation against the practice of torture.

Given the accumulating evidence that torture may be practised persistently by public servants in Israel, we call on the state to initiate a broad and explicit counteractive campaign. The practice of violence and cruelty by public servants upon persons in custody, placed totally at their mercy, must be singled out as an especially grave breach of the moral principles of democratic government, punishable by severe measures. In the absence of express legislation against torture this message is absent from Israel's code of law. Yet, at present no existing Israeli law deals expressly and specifically with torture.

Israel, as a member of the United Nations, is signatory to international conventions and declarations against torture, including the United Nations Convention on Protection of All Persons from Torture and Other Cruel, Inhuman or Degrading Treatment or Punishment, 1975, and the subsequent Convention, in fact ratified by Israel in 1991. We call upon the Israeli legislator to incorporate these into Israeli domestic law. We call on the state to eradicate any existing ambiguity attached to the full application of this law and the relevant international conventions to all territories and persons under Israel's rule.

Pending such legislation and in keeping with the UN Convention, we urge the immediate initiation of independent investigation of reports of torture and publication of the findings. Neither of the two Knesset (Parliament) subcommittees presently responsible for public supervision of the main interrogating authorities in Israel has published any report or account of its activities since its appointment. We hereby call on the State of Israel to take action towards rendering its agencies and employees fully and publicly accountable for the practice of torture.

IV   Proposal for an addendum to the Israeli Medical Association's Code of Ethics

The following proposal for an addendum to the Israeli Medical Association's Code of Ethics was debated and formulated by the Board of Directors of the Association of Israeli-Palestinian Physicians for Human Rights. It is presented here in English, translated from the original Hebrew text.

Foreword to the PHR Proposal for an Addendum to the IMA Code of Ethics

The Association of Israeli-Palestinian Physicians for Human Rights (PHR) sees the following proposal (for an addendum to the IMA code of ethics) as an important means for realizing the special role which PHR ascribes to physicians in preventing breaches of human rights in jails and preventing the torture of persons in custody or under interrogation.

The Israeli Medical Association (IMA) has endorsed the Tokyo Declaration against torture adopted by the World Medical Association in 1975. The members of PHR believe that adoption of the addendum by the IMA will constitute a central step towards translation of that important declaration into practice in Israel. Clear and detailed guidelines for professional conduct in the practical reality in which IMA member physicians find themselves, form an essential tie between the declarative and the applicative levels.

In formulating the proposal, we looked to the law prohibiting the abuse of minors and the defenseless, due to the clear parallel between the circumstances of children in the custody of, and at the mercy of, parents and the circumstances of prisoners or detainees in the custody of, and at the mercy of, the state and the people responsible for guarding them. In both cases the child or prisoner is exposed to possible violent attack(s) by their custodians, while their special status makes them defenseless against such harm. For this reason, the state and society of Israel have undertaken to provide minors and the defenseless with special external protection. Following legislation to this effect in 1989, there has been a considerable increase in the number of reports of abuse of minors. This in turn has enhanced opportunities for intervention by the relevant authorities towards ending such situations. The new law includes an important clause imposing a duty to report upon any person encountering evidence of the abuse of minors or defenseless persons. Indeed, the law imposes punishment on those failing to fulfill this duty. Moreover, the punishments imposed on care professionals such as physicians, social workers or teachers who fail to fulfill this duty are twice as severe as those imposed on others. The law thus places a special responsibility on the care professions for safeguarding the well-being of minors and the defenseless.

A prisoner, who is potentially exposed to factors such as hostile public opinion, racism, desire for revenge, is no less – and perhaps more – at risk from violence on the part of his or her custodians and interrogators. We therefore propose that a physician treating or encountering a person in the custody of the state be doubly alert to the possibility of violence against that person. In the absence of clear legislation obligating physicians to report evidence of such violence, we propose the introduction of an obligation to report to a special IMA body to be established for this express purpose. It is further proposed that the IMA act concurrently to promote legislation imposing a duty to report to state institutions, comparable to the duty to report the abuse of minors or the defenseless.

In addition, the proposed addendum incorporates a series of guidelines aimed at preventing the possible utilization of physicians by custodian authorities for abuse of the prisoner or his/her basic rights. The proposal sets out a detailed code of professional conduct necessary for the correct implementation of the principles of medical ethics.

Proposal for an addendum to the IMA Code of Ethics
Introduction

The physician's first duty is to his or her patient. When a conflict arises between the interest of safeguarding the physical and mental health of a person in custody and the interests of the custodian authorities, it is the duty of the physician to act for the good and in the interest of the physical and mental integrity of the patient without applying other considerations of any kind. Loss of liberty does not imply loss of right to medical care.

Comment on terminology used in this text

The term 'prison' encompasses all detention facilities, including police stations, military camps, and interrogation centers.

The term 'torture' includes torture and all other cruel, inhuman and degrading treatment or punishment.

The term 'Prisoner' applies to all persons held in some form of detention, pre-trial detainees, convicted prisoners, administrative detainees.

The term 'Physician' applies to all physicians working inside or outside prison facilities, who consult, treat, monitor, or observe prisoners.

Part 1 Preventing medical negligence or defective medical treatment for persons in custody

1. A Physician called upon to treat a Prisoner, whether inside or outside a prison facility, will obtain the express consent of the Prisoner before administering any tests or treatment. Prisoners consenting to treatment must be free from any form of pressure or coercion. When the Prisoner's express consent cannot be obtained (when he/she is unconscious, for example), the Physician will act upon considerations identical to those which would guide him/her for a patient outside a prison facility, that is only in the Prisoner's best interest.

2. A Physician will verify that every Prisoner receive a medical examination within 48 hours of the Prisoner's arrival in the prison, as stipulated in prison

regulations. A Physician will also examine every Prisoner within 48 hours after the transfer of the Prisoner to any other place.

3. A Physician called upon to treat a Prisoner (whether inside or outside a prison facility) will provide the Prisoner with medical treatment identical to the treatment customarily given to any free patient in similar medical condition. The Physician will not restrict the treatment or order its postponement until after the Prisoner's release.

4. A Physician will obtain all the information regarding the Prisoner's medical history, with the consent of the Prisoner. This includes contacting the Prisoner's former Physician, with the Prisoner's consent.

5. Where the medical staff of a prison facility are unable to provide the Prisoner with full treatment or expert consultation, the Physician in charge will refer the Prisoner to a health facility outside the prison and provide the outside expert with all the medical information necessary for the Prisoner's diagnosis and treatment. This information shall be provided promptly upon referral and with the consent of the Prisoner.

6. Where a Prisoner is examined and/or treated at his/her own request or that of his family, by a Physician who is not employed by the Security Forces or the Prison Services, the prison facility Physician in charge will cooperate fully with the examining/treating Physician and present him/her with all the medical documents concerning the Prisoner.

7. Where a Prisoner needs constant medical supervision, surgical procedure or professional assistance in fulfilling basic needs, the Physician in charge will transfer him/her without delay to the prison clinic or to a medical center outside the prison, as is required by the severity of the Prisoner's condition.

8. The Physician in charge of the Prisoner's health will respond in detail and within a reasonable time to requests for medical information referred to him by the Prisoner's immediate family or his/her legal representative, subject to the written consent or refusal of the patient-Prisoner. If it is impossible to obtain consent (because the Prisoner is unconscious for example), the medical officers must be guided only by considerations of the Prisoner's best interest.

9. A Physician with reason to believe that a certain Prisoner is not being provided with medical treatment as aforesaid, will report the matter to the IMA at the earliest opportunity and within no more than 15 days or immediately in emergency situations. Furthermore, a Physician coming across evidence of breaches of the above or present paragraphs on the part of a colleague, will report the matter to the IMA at the earliest opportunity and within no more than 15 days or immediately in emergency situations.

Part 2 Prohibiting participation in torture and imposing a duty to report torture

1. Torture contradicts the basic principles of medical ethics. As stipulated in the Tokyo Declaration of the World Medical Association in 1975, adopted in its entirety by the IMA, Physicians are forbidden to 'countenance, condone or participate in the practice of torture or other forms of cruel, inhuman or degrading procedures, whatever the offence of which the victim of such pro-

cedures is suspected, accused or guilty, and whatever the victim's beliefs or motives, and in all situations, including armed conflict and civil strife'.

2. A Physician encountering evidence of acts of physical or mental cruelty or degradation towards a person in custody, will take practical steps to prevent or end them. Such steps include the obligation of the Physician to address an immediate protest to the warden of the prison facility. This duty applies to every Physician encountering such evidence, for example, during treatment of a Prisoner in a hospital or clinic outside the prison, or during military reserve service in a military detention center. In addition, the Physician will report to the IMA on the evidence which he/she has encountered, at the earliest opportunity or within 5 days at most.

Physicians' reports will be submitted to a special department (hotline) of the IMA Ethics Bureau, whose function will be their receival, consulting the reporting Physicians on their consequent ethical conduct, and taking urgent action on the incoming reports (as detailed in Part 4).

3. A Physician with reason to believe that the conduct of a colleague is in breach of one or more of the above paragraphs, will report the matter to the IMA at the earliest opportunity or within 5 days at most.

Part 3 Retaining medical independence and preventing participation in torture

In order to retain his/her medical independence and refrain from involvement in actions contradicting medical ethics, every Physician will take care to observe the following rules:

1. The Physician will demand direct and confidential contact with any Prisoner he/she treats. The Physician will insist that no medical examination or treatment be performed in the presence of a third party who might restrict free contact or affect normal doctor–patient relations, except in special cases when the Physician requests the presence of a third party for his/her protection or for similar purposes, and makes that request in writing. A Physician forced to provide urgent medical treatment despite non-fulfillment of this demand, will report the matter to the IMA at the earliest opportunity or within 5 days at most.

2. A Physician (male) asked to examine or treat a female Prisoner will demand the presence of an additional woman during the examination and/or treatment. A Physician forced to administer urgent treatment despite non-fulfillment of this demand, will report the matter to the IMA at the earliest opportunity or within 5 days at most.

3. Prior to examination or treatment of a Prisoner, the Physician will ascertain that these will be provided in conditions allowing for the free and independent arrival at, and implementation of, his/her clinical decisions concerning the patient, guided only by considerations of the patient's best interests. A Physician forced to perform an examination or treatment despite his/her uncertainty of the existence of such conditions, will report the matter to the IMA at the earliest opportunity or within 5 days at most.

4. The Physician will make detailed and precise records of the findings of

each medical examination and a detailed and precise report on any medical treatment he/she administers to a Prisoner, in proper and orderly form including his/her own full identification as administering Physician, in clear and legible handwriting. The Physician will ensure that each medical document is kept in the Prisoner's medical file and that the medical file remains confidential. A Physician prevented from accurately documenting and keeping his/her findings will report the matter to the IMA at the earliest opportunity or within 5 days at most.

5. If the Prisoner is making an allegation of torture, before a court or other authority, the Physician will make the complete and truthful medical file accessible to the Prisoner or to his/her lawyer with the Prisoner's consent.

6. Prior to any examination or treatment of a Prisoner, the administering Physician will identify him/herself to the Prisoner, giving his/her full name and position. The Physician may not in any circumstances refuse to provide the Prisoner with his/her identifying details. A Physician requested by any authority not to identify him/herself to a Prisoner, or a Physician forced to administer urgent medical treatment despite having been forbidden to identify him/herself, will report the matter to the IMA at the earliest opportunity or within 5 days at most. The Prisoner will also be identified to the Physician.

7. The Physician will demand that during his/her administration of examinations, treatment or medical services, the patient-Prisoner not be blindfolded or otherwise prevented from seeing him/her (unless eye covering is required for medical reasons). A Physician asked to do so or forced to administer urgent treatment to a Prisoner prevented from seeing him/her, will report the matter to the IMA at the earliest opportunity or within 5 days at most.

8. A Physician shall not perform procedures of any kind which are not required for a Prisoner's medical needs. A Physician will not provide information facilitating interrogation, as his/her duties are towards the patient-Prisoner and not towards the interrogators. If the Prisoner cannot undergo interrogation, it is the Physician's duty to inform the prison authorities immediately. A Physician will in no event provide assessments or fill out forms detailing the Prisoner's ability to withstand torture. A Physician forced, for fear of his/her own wellbeing, to perform such procedures or provide such information, will report the matter to the IMA at the earliest opportunity or within 5 days at most.

9. A Physician deferring the provision of medical services so as to refrain from complicity in a breach of the patient's rights, will report the deferral and the reasons for it to the IMA within 5 days at most from the date of his/her refusal. At the time of the deferral, the Physician will explain the reason for his/her decision to the Prisoner. In no case will the Physician defer urgent and vital medical treatment.

10. The Physician will not be partner to a refusal to answer a need for medical treatment or nursing, or assistance in other vital needs of a Prisoner, where that need is expressed explicitly or concluded in another way.

Part 4 Role of the physician during hunger-strike of a prisoner

1. When a Prisoner refuses nourishment (hunger-strike) and is considered by a Physician as capable of forming an unimpaired and rational judgment

concerning the consequences of such voluntary refusal of nourishment, he/she shall not be fed artificially. A Physician shall clearly inform the Prisoner, at the beginning of the strike, that he/she will not be resuscitated unless he/she expresses a change of mind and a wish not to die as a result of the hunger-strike. If there is any doubt about a Prisoner's intentions to continue the hunger-strike till death, the Physician must strive to do the best for that Prisoner. This might involve resuscitation if the prisoner's views are unknown. If it is clear the prisoner intended to continue the strike until death, he/she must be allowed to die in dignity.

2. A Physician who feels unable for reasons of conscience, or for any other reason, to abide by the prisoner's decision must allow another Physician to supervise care.

Part 5 The duties of the IMA in preventing medical complicity in torture

1. The IMA will found and staff a special department (hotline) of the Ethics Bureau, whose function will be to receive reports from Physicians on the breach of one or more of the above paragraphs, to consult the reporting Physicians on their consequent ethical conduct, and take urgent action on the incoming reports. This special department will also be able to receive reports from non-physicians, such as Prisoners, their families, lawyers, and human rights organizations, regarding the conduct of Physicians.

2. Where a Physician's report under one of the above paragraphs raises a reasonable suspicion that a criminal offense has been committed by an official authority, the department, on behalf of the IMA, will apply to the relevant state authorities in demand for an inquiry into the complaint and receival of an adequate reply within a reasonable time. Where the report raises a suspicion of immediate and/or grave risk to the life or health of a Prisoner, this application will be made with maximal urgency or within 3 days at most of receipt of the report. The IMA will brief the reporting Physician on its handling of the issue.

3. The IMA department will give advice and answer queries presented to it by individual Physicians regarding how they should react in conformity with medical ethics, to difficult decisions and positions which confront them in their work. The IMA will offer formal support (such as a letter) to the ethical conduct of the Physician.

4. Where a Physician employed at a prison facility is required to breach his/her medical independence or the principles of medical ethics, the IMA will refer directly to the warden of the facility demanding an investigation and an end to the breach.

5. Where the job of a Physician employed in a prison facility is terminated or impaired in such circumstances, or where a threat to this effect arises, the IMA will provide that Physician with legal assistance as necessary.

6. In exceptional cases, the IMA will consider authorizing that the identity of a Physician reporting under one of the above paragraphs be kept confidential.

7. The IMA will take the disciplinary measures available to it against a Physician found to have breached one of the above paragraphs.

PHR Recommendations to the IMA for action to end torture

1. The IMA will adopt an ethical code for Physicians treating Prisoners and detainees.

2. The IMA will see to the distribution of the ethical code and the principles upon which it rests, among its membership, the medical community in general and the general public. In particular, the IMA will see to the distribution of the code of ethics and its principles among those Physicians serving in prison facilities.

3. The IMA will act to teach in medical schools all the details of the medical ethics that guide the treatment of Prisoners and detainees, and will conduct periodic courses on this subject for Physicians serving in prison facilities.

4. The IMA will found and staff a hotline for receiving reports of evidence of the torture or medical neglect of Prisoners, as detailed in Part 4 of the addendum: The Duties of the IMA in Preventing Medical Involvement in Torture.

5. The IMA will set up and operate a working group for investigating the involvement of Physicians in interrogations in Israel. The group will publish its findings within a stipulated time.

6. The IMA will propose and promote a regulation instructing the direct subordination of Physicians working in prison facilities to the Ministry of Health, rather than the prison authorities.

7. The IMA will act to promote legislation imposing on Physicians a duty to report to state authorities any evidence of torture that may come to their knowledge, analogous to their duty to report evidence of child abuse.

8. The IMA will act to establish and apply the right of every Prisoner to receive a medical opinion from an external Physician, independent of the prison authorities.

9. The IMA will promote the formulation of similar addenda regarding torture to the Codes of Ethics of other associations of health professionals.

v Evidence of torture in Israel: affidavits of survivors

Despite Israel's ratification of the UN Convention against Torture and Other Cruel, Inhuman or Degrading Treatment or Punishment, of 1984, the use of torture is still an accepted weapon used by the state. Numerous affidavits evidencing torture exist. Those presented here were chosen on the basis of the manner by which they evidence the different forms of torture sanctioned and utilized by the state prior to the Intifada and continuing into the present day. In the first affidavit, a pregnant woman describes the torture she endured which resulted in the loss of her child. In the second, a 12-year-old boy describes his experiences of torture. Two brothers, in affidavits 3 and 4, tell how they were detained and tortured by collaborators. One brother is forced to implicate the other and confess to crimes he did not commit. Affidavits 5 and 6 not only testify to the brutality of the General Security Services (GSS) but also expose the different methods of torture that the GSS has established.

We decided to maintain the authenticity of the affidavits and regret that the language is colloquial.

Affidavit 1 March 16, 1987

I, the undersigned, Naila Ibrahim Othman Al Iyadi (A'yesh), after having been warned by Advocate Felicia Langer that I must testify truthfully or be liable to punishment as stated by the law, hereby testify the following:

1. I hereby testify about my pregnancy, about the loss of my child, and about all the relevant details as follows:

a. I told my interrogators from the beginning that I am pregnant, to which they replied: 'You are like a man and there is no difference about that, and it does not matter to us.'

b. Beginning from 21.2.87 my interrogators put a bag [of cloth] over my head for a long period and I was outside in bitter cold. This was repeated several times.

c. The interrogators cursed me and threatened to undress me. One of them – tall, light hair, with protruding eyes – slammed my head against the wall. The interrogators (usually three and sometimes four) would curse me. I felt like an object of play – as if they divided the roles among themselves: one would curse me, one would hit, one pretended he wanted to help.

d. I told the investigator who hit me (slammed my head against a wall) that he should be ashamed to hit a pregnant woman. At that time I had already started hemorrhaging, and I told this to the investigators, that they had killed my child, and asking if they wanted to kill me too?

e. I did not receive any medical treatment, despite my pleas, and my feeling very sick, and my complaints concerning that. Once, on the 25th or 26th of

February (and this although I had been detained on the 19th of February and had been asking for a doctor since then) a person introducing himself as a doctor came to me. I complained about my situation, yet he did not help or treat me, but ordered to have me make a urine test. The doctor came in the presence of the investigators and did not examine me. The next day I gave a urine test, and it was mixed with blood.

f. My questions concerning the test results, while I was still bleeding, were not answered. One of the interrogators told me after begging, about five days after the test, that nothing was wrong with me. Now I doubt that the man who posed as a doctor was indeed a doctor.

g. The interrogators told me at the beginning that I would see a doctor only after I confessed. Only when I confessed so as to put an end to the torture, was I allowed to change my clothes.

h. The interrogators also did not believe that I suffered from terrible pains in my stomach, and when I put my hand on my stomach they would shout: 'Take your hands off your stomach!' I would vomit and they would say 'You're acting!' and this happened several times. My explanations about the nausea I was suffering from did not help.

i. When they would return me to my room [cell] it was specially cooled by an airconditioner.

j. Only on March 15, after countless requests and demands to be examined by a doctor and receive his aid, was I brought to a prison doctor: the doctor interrogated me and did not examine me, and those who were present in the room denied that I was pregnant and that I had told them this and claimed, something which is a complete lie, that I am hemorrhaging and nothing more, and that I only asked for cotton swabs.

k. I was returned to my cell and about three hours later I was brought, with my hands tied, to Hadassa Ein Kerem, and from there to another hospital, they said because there was no doctor in Hadassah.

l. I was taken out in a police car, handcuffed, with a policewoman and a medic or a doctor who used to register my name in the Russian Compound Jail.

m. The Kupat Holim doctor (I don't know where) gave me a gynecological examination. After the examination was over the medic or doctor from the prison entered and they talked between themselves for half an hour. I understood from the voice of the doctor that he was angry. I asked the policewoman what they were talking about and asked her to translate for me. She promised she would do so after we left the place.

n. After we left I asked her what they talked about at the gynecologist's. She said she hadn't heard a thing. The doctor spoke to me in English and gave me an urgent appointment for 16.3 and for Tuesday 17.3 for an ultrasound test and a blood test.

o. My questions about the results of the examination were not answered, despite my repeated requests.

I hereby declare that my interrogators and those in charge of the prison are responsible for the loss of my child and for all the possible consequences regarding my fertility. Moreover, if they had listened to my pleas and brought a doctor from the beginning, it may have been possible to save my child despite the hemorrhage I mentioned.

I now suffer from physical weakness and depression due to all that had happened to me and due to the inhuman treatment to which I testified above.

Everything stated in this testimony is true and correct.

Signature of the testifier Naila Ibrahim
Russian Compound Prison

Affidavit 2 November 1, 1989

I, the undersigned, after being warned that I must state the truth or else be liable to the punishment stated by the law, hereby declare in writing as follows:

1. My name is Morad Jadallah, I am twelve years and nine months old.

2. I was arrested on Sunday, 29.10.89, on a street in Beit Safafa. It was 7:00 in the morning.

3. They took me to a Ford van, ordered me to kneel and bend my knees and my back, as well as my head, and the policemen (three of them) kicked with their legs at my head and my back.

4. They took me to the Russian Compound and started to interrogate me. The interrogators came over to me. They were seven people and started to beat me with a club on my legs and my body and demanded that I tell them about the activity of other children. However I didn't tell them anything. I was not asked about myself, only about the other children.

5. I had marks on my face as the result of the blows, which can still be seen today, but on Sunday they looked worse and my face was swollen.

6. On the day I was taken to court, Tuesday, 31.10.89, I told Advocate Walid Zakhalka that I had been beaten during interrogation and showed him the mark on my face [swelling on the right side] as I show you now, during the recording of the testimony.

7. I don't know if the advocate complained before the judge because I don't speak Hebrew.

8. My Father saw me, but was forbidden to speak with me after we left the judge. In front of the judge, who extended my detention for another four days, I denied knowing the children and did not confess to anything.

9. After they took me back to interrogation an interrogator who speaks Arabic, tall, interrogated me and didn't beat me; in the interrogation room there were four interrogators and three of them started to beat me, while I was ordered to stand next to the wall; one of them is tall, wears glasses, black hair, his age is about 35; the second is fat, taller than the first, his hair is short and black; the third was short or of medium height, his hair isn't black nor blond (light brown) and he spat at me, on my face.

10. One of them banged my head on the table and the others beat me on my thighs; I still held up but shouted out of pain, but they ordered me to shut up; the fat man would beat me more than the others on my body, with a club.

11. Later they brought a boy, about 13 years old, and said that he had incriminated me in a confession about me. The interrogators told me that I have to confess because everybody confesses. They told me that there's a short

way, that is the way of confession, and the long way, which is the way of the club. The interrogator said that they would destroy the family home and arrest my father if I didn't confess. They showed me my aunt whom I love and said that she had been arrested while she was visiting me. They put her in a room and lied to me and I know that now. (They said) that she was arrested, seemingly, because of me and that I'm the cause for the detention of the one who cared for me for seven years, because I don't have a conscience and confess. That was on the first day of my detention and all of this after they asked me who I love more, my father or my aunt.

12. After the beatings and the threats and the confrontation with the other child I confessed to having participated in three demonstrations. I was very tired due to the beatings and was afraid that they would take revenge on my family, as they threatened me.

13. Yesterday, after I was severely beaten, I asked for medical treatment and then I was told that only after I confess can I receive medical treatment.

14. When I complained why they are beating me and that it is forbidden, they told me that I'm a terrorist in the Democratic Front, or responsible for the Fatah, or the Popular Front and hit me in the face. The manner of the beating was such: one of them pulled my hair at the temples and the second one, called Musa, would slap me many times on the cheeks. They told me: 'You're small but you're laughing at everyone.'

My whole body hurt, especially my head; it's hard for me to lie down because of the pain and I couldn't sleep. Even today I asked Adv. Zakhalka to make them give me medical treatment, carry out an X-ray, because I feel pains all over my body.

I ask you to complain about what they did to me and everything stated in this testimony is true and correct.

Testifier's signature

The above-mentioned testifier appeared before me in the detention center for minors at the Russian Compound and was identified by those who brought him to me and by himself and after being warned as stated by law he signed the above testimony, after confirming its truth.

Adv. Felicia Langer

Affadavit 3 February 11, 1990

I, the undersigned, Ali Ibrahim El-Gul, after being warned that I must speak the truth and knowing that I will be punished according to the law if I neglect to do so, hereby declare:

1. I am twenty-five years old, married and father of triplets, who are one year old. I work as a handyman in Jerusalem.

2. I was arrested on Saturday December 16, 1989. I was taken from my house at 10:30 at night and brought to the Russian Compound.

3. The police from the 'minority wing' tied my hands behind my back and began slapping me in the face. They threw me to the floor, took off my shoes, and tied my eyes with a shirt that was on the floor and then began hitting the

soles of my feet. I'm pretty sure that they were hitting me with clubs. My attackers did not make themselves known and they were not the interrogators. I think that I would be able to indentify them if I were to see them again.

The beating continued until three in the morning, after which an interrogator, whose name was Yosi Ben-Yair, told me that I was suspected of attempting the murder of Abdallah Mashal. He told me that I was being detained for forty-eight hours.

4. I was taken into solitary confinement, cell #120. The following morning I was once again taken to the 'minority wing'. An interrogator named Ahmad Trudy informed me that I was suspected of murder and that my brother had already implicated me. He flashed me a document written in Hebrew.

5. On Monday, December 18, 1989, a judge extended my detention. The whole process lasted about a minute. I told the judge that I had been beaten and he asked if there were any marks. When I said there were none, the judge told me that my brother had confessed and he extended my detention for fifteen days. I was taken from the court to the 'minority wing'. I was left standing and tied up for several hours. My requests for water and to go to the bathroom were refused. Afterwards, I was interrogated and I denied all the accusations. I was sent to wait.

6. At approximately five in the afternoon, Ahmad Trudy came back to where I was being held and blindfolded me with a kafia. My hands were already tied. He told me, 'If you do not confess, I don't care if they come to hit you.' After a minute or two, they took off my shoes and hit the soles of my feet – I screamed from the pain. I was left there, lying on the floor, until approximately eight in the evening. Later, they returned and hit me on the soles of my feet. The unidentified person that had hit me then helped me up and tied something to the metal handcuff I had behind my back. He tied me so that he could lift my hands into a painful position – onto something I thought was a doorhandle. Every quarter of an hour Ahmad Trudy would come and ask me if I was ready to confess. This continued for approximately two hours. I felt like my hands had frozen and began shouting and kicking the door. Ahmad Trudy came running and took off the rope and the handcuffs and took me to be interrogated. This session lasted for approximately an hour. I denied all of the allegations brought up against me. They put me into a lawyer's room in the detention chambers until the next morning.

7. The following morning, at approximately nine, I was taken again to the 'minority wing'. My head was hooded and my hands were tied behind my back and were still connected to a cupboard. I was made to sit on a carton. After about two hours I was again hit on the soles of my feet and on my buttocks with a club. Again I was tied to the cupboard. This continued until about two in the afternoon. I pulled my hands and the cupboard fell on my back. Ahmad walked in and untied me but kept me seated on the carton with my hands behind my back. An hour later Ahmad returned and told me that he must now go and he was leaving me with 'the bad guys' and that they would hit me. And just as he said, the beating continued after he left. Again it was on the soles of my feet and on my buttocks. At approximately five p.m., Ahmad Trudy returned and

asked me, once again, to confess. He threatened to call the people that had hit me if I didn't confess. He left. After he left I heard people screaming (all during that day I was hooded) and they took me to another room where they hit me harder than they had hit me before – on my hands, on my buttocks, and on my legs. They hit me until I lost all sensation. Ahmad Trudy arrived and untied me and took off the hood from my head and gave me some food. I was returned to solitary confinement.

8. From Tuesday, December 19, 1989 until Sunday the 24th, I was not interrogated. On Sunday at approximately three p.m. I was brought to the GSS wing. There I was interrogated by a man named Major Roni. Major Roni showed me a confession written in Arabic by my brother (as Roni said) and pictures in which our alleged crime was reconstructed. After this interrogation, I was taken to what seemed to be a storage room. There I was tied to a chair for around two hours and later taken to a small cell. There two detainees talked with me.

9. The next morning, Monday, I was taken back into solitary confinement. On Tuesday, December 26, 1989 Ahmad Trudy arrived and took me to the 'minority wing'. There he told me that my brother had also confessed to the murder of Halil Karin and that he had claimed I was his accomplice. I denied these accusations. At that moment, he tied my hands behind my back and began slapping my face. He grabbed my head and twisted it from side to side with all his strength and gave me two blows with his fingers on my throat. He grabbed my head and threw me to the floor. After I was thrown on the floor another person came into the room and blindfolded me (until then I could see all of Trudy's movements). They started banging my head against the floor and I knew that Trudy was still there because I could identify his Reebok shoes. They stepped on my face every time that I began to shout. They began hitting my head with a hard object while I was still lying on the floor. I also received two blows on my shoulders with that same object. I felt breathless from those last blows. Immediately they took off my handcuffs and my hood. I saw Trudy and another person named Ilan standing there and I saw that Ahmad wore Reebok shoes and I saw on the floor a thick electricity cable. Ahmad took the cable and hid it. I put my hands on my head and felt that my head and lips were swollen. Ahmad gave me water to drink and let me rest for an hour. After that, he brought me back to an isolated cell.

10. Immediately after I arrived in the cell, I fainted and when I woke up I asked permission to see a medic. The medic came and took me to the infirmary where he examined my head and chest, because I told him that I could not breathe. He told me that it was just superficial damage and that my heart was not damaged. He gave me a pain reliever called Maxsol. I told him that my condition was due to the blows that I had received from the interrogation. He asked me if I would like him to document the fact that I had been beaten. I told him I would tell everything to my lawyer.

11. I was in my room until Wednesday evening. On Wednesday evening the medic arrived and saw that my eyes were swollen. He told me that we would wait until the next morning to see how my condition developed. On Thursday

December 28, my eyes were even more swollen and my right eye looked like an egg. The medic called the doctor, who decided that I should be transferred to the hospital. A police officer from the prison took me to Haddasah Ein Karem Hospital where my eye was examined. The doctor told me that my eye was okay but that the blows that I received were affecting my head. I told my doctor that I had received blows from the interrogators during interrogation. He wrote a letter to the prison doctor and the policeman took the letter with him. I never saw the contents of the letter.

12. After that I was not interrogated for a week. On January 1, 1990, I complained to my lawyer and she complained to Judge Hashin who had extended my detention for fifteen days. On the way from the courthouse, Ilan told me that I would not go back to the hospital but to an insane asylum and Yossi continued and said, 'not to an insane asylum but to a cemetery'.

13. On Thursday January 4, 1990, Ahmad Trudy, Yossi Ben-Yair, Ilan, and Moti walked into my cell and took me and my cousin Monir. They told us that we were going for a medical examination at Abu-Kabir prison. However, we did not reach the prison because there was a bomb threat.

14. On January 15, 1990, the police decided to try us at the military court at Lod. The police accused us of throwing Molotov cocktails and notified the court that they were still investigating the accusations of murder. In any case, they claimed, they could not try us for murder at the military court at Lod. My detention was extended until February 5, 1990, at which time it was extended until further notice.

15. On February 7, I was released from detention. I was told that I was released because they had discovered the person who had actually committed the crimes of throwing the Molotov cocktails, the murder and the attempted murder.

16. This affidavit has been given so that it can be presented to any institution and any person.

17. I declare that this is my name, this is my signature and the content of the affidavit is true.

Signature of Ali Ibrahim El-Gul

Today, February 11, 1990, I, Attorney Lea Tsemel, met Ali Ibrahim El-Gul, I.D. 8031775 in my offices. After I warned him that he must speak the truth and made him aware that he would be punished according to the law if he failed to do so, he swore to the truth of his statements.

Signature of Lea Tsemel

Affidavit 4 February 9, 1990

I, the undersigned, Ismail Ibrahim Musa El-Gul, after being warned that I must speak the truth and knowing that I will be punished according to the law if I neglect to do so, hereby declare:

1. I live in Silwan neighborhood in Jerusalem. I am twenty-two years old and work as an electrician.

2. I was arrested on December 16, 1989 at 22:30 from my house, after my house had been thoroughly searched.

3. Immediately after my arrest, I was brought to the 'minority wing' in the Russian Compound. I was held standing with my hands tied behind my back until two in the morning. At that point, they began interrogating me and I denied their accusations against me, accusations concerning the knife assault on Abdallah Mashal. One of the interrogators introduced himself as Yosef Avraham while the other, a young man, did not introduce himself at all.

4. After I denied the accusations, I was beaten by these two men in different ways. They focused on hitting the soles of my feet with a club and after that they had made me take off my shoes. They hit the soles of my feet and poured cold water on me. Evidence that cold water had been used has to do with the sweater I was wearing. It was close to seven in the morning when I broke my resolve and began collaborating; my interrogators took off the sweater I was wearing and it was soaked with water. They put the sweater on the heater so that it would dry. The sweater was burned and it changed color from the heat. I showed the sweater to my attorney and to two judges.

5. As a result of the beatings and the cold, I confessed to assaulting Abdallah Mashal with a knife. The interrogator, who had introduced himself as Yosef Avraham, wrote a confession in my name and in Arabic. I signed it. My confession took place at approximately eight in the morning and I implicated two other people, one of whom I named – Adnan Majarah, the other I claimed that I did not know and that Adnan had brought him along.

6. About 11:30 the same morning, I was interrogated by someone named Ahmad Trudy. Because I was unwilling to collaborate with Trudy, he threatened to take me back to the two other people who had interrogated me during the night. He knew that I had been beaten and I told him myself that I had been beaten.

7. Ahmad Trudy brought up a new accusation to which I also confessed. The case of someone throwing a Molotov cocktail on the house of Majid Jaber. I confessed because Trudy threatened to take me back to the two other interrogators if I did not.

8. Trudy took another confession, different from the first one that I gave. In this statement, I confessed that other than myself and Adnan, my brother, Ali, took part in the stabbing. I also confessed that Adnan and Ali participated in throwing the Molotov cocktail on the house of Majid Jaber.

9. To the best of my memory, on December 18, 1989, I was brought to a judge so that my detention could be extended. I was so scared that I did not tell the judge that I had been beaten. I did ask for a lawyer.

10. On a date that I do not remember, I was taken out of detention to reconstruct the scenes of the confessions I had made. I pointed out, to the best of my knowledge, the places where I had supposedly committed crimes. During this time Trudy corrected me several times because my statements were not correct or logical. I allowed myself to be corrected – using his directives.

During this time Trudy also interrogated me about the death of Khallil, but I denied having been involved in this.

11. On December 27, 1989, at 18:30, I was taken out of solitary confinement. My head was covered by a kafia and my hands were tied behind my back. I was brought to the 'minority wing' where I was beaten continually with clubs on the soles of my feet for two hours. After which my kafia was taken off and I saw Ahmad Trudy. He asked me, 'Who took you out of the cell?' and he started yelling at the policemen. 'Who took him out of the room?' he asked again. From his expression it was clear that he was acting. He made it seem as if he didn't know what had happened so that he could not be suspected of participating in my beatings. Everyone answered that they did not know who had taken me out of the cell.

12. Ahmad Trudy then told me that we were not the three people who had commited the crimes. I volunteered the names of my cousin Monir El-Gul and Izam El-Gul as if they had been with us. He interrogated me about the murder of Halil Karin and I denied that I had participated in the murder. During this interrogation I asked him to bring witnesses. I asked him to bring my sister Hodah; I was at her house at the time of Halil Karin's murder. I also asked him to bring Amar, the brother of my sister's husband, who had seen me at my sister's house. From time to time, I asked him to bring in the wife of Abdallah Mashal because I had heard that she had seen the person who had assaulted her husband and could testify that I had not done it. I must note, that every once in a while, I told Trudy that my confessions were lies and demanded that the witnesses be brought forth. He would answer, 'Okay, first make a false confession about the murder.'

13. I was taken back to solitary confinement. Trudy promised that on Thursday he would call my sister so that she could testify on my behalf. However, I was not taken out of confinement once on Thursday. I was alone all day in my cell.

14. On Friday December 29, 1989, I was taken out of my cell in the morning. Again Trudy threatened that I would be taken back to the people who had beaten me if I did not confess, and from fear, I confessed. I also understood that he had not brought my sister as he had promised. I confessed to the murder of Halil Karin and I stated that all four people that I had mentioned before participated in the murder. I gave a detailed description of Karin's murder: how I had participated in it, how he was hit with an axe, how I saw Adnan with a knife in his hand and how I saw that inscribed into Karin's chest was 'This Is A Collaborator'. I would like to add that while I was being held in confinement, I was taken out once and put together with a person who had introduced himself as Muhsain Abu-Diab. He told me that Karin was found with an inscription on his chest that read: 'This Is A Collaborator'.

After I made this last confession I asked Trudy to transfer me from my cell because I could not stand it any longer. After giving the statement I was transferred to Beit Shemesh.

15. The following day, Saturday, I was brought back to Jerusalem to my cousin Monir. When I saw him, I said in front of the interrogators, that I had made a false confession due to the torture I had been subjected to and due to my disturbed mental condition. We were left alone and it was only recently that I understood that our conversation had been recorded. All the people who hear

the recordings will understand that neither of us had taken any part in any of the acts we were accused of being involved in.

16. I was taken back to Beit Shemesh where I was detained until my imprisonment was extended by Judge Hashin on January 1, 1990. I stayed there for more than the necessary time.

17. My attorney saw me for the first time at the court on January 1, 1990. I found out from her that she had tried to visit me herself and that she had even sent Attorney Sha'aban to visit me a few times. Every time they had offerred different excuses for denying me the visits. I told her that my confessions were false and that the reconstructions of the scenes were also false. I was mentally unstable and I could not stop crying. My family and my attorney all saw this. My attorney gave the details of my torture and interrogation to the court. Although my attorney asked the court to reduce my imprisonment so that it could monitor the legality of my interrogation, my imprisonment was extended for fifteen days.

18. After the trial I was sent back to Beit Shemesh and my interrogation did not resume.

19. On January 15, 1990, I was brought in front of the Judge Prokachia. The state requested that my case be transfered to the Military Court in Lod so that I could be tried for the crime of throwing a Molotov cocktail. The prosecutor claimed that the interrogation concerning the murder was still going on but that in the meantime they preferred to file a partial suit. My imprisonment was extended for another eight days. At Lod my imprisonment was extended after seven days and later, on February 5, 1990, my attorney denied the accusations brought against me and asked the court to allow a 'mini-trial'.

20. On February 6, 1990, while I was in the Russian Compound a police interrogator took me to the 'minority wing' where he asked me if in exchange for 'cancelling' my confessions, I would implicate Adnan. After I told him that I didn't know where Adnan was, he took a confession from me in which I denied the legitimacy of all of my prior confessions. To the question why I had given false confessions, I told him that I had given these as a result of my torture and confinement. When I was questioned as to why I had given the names of my friends, I told them that only my friends could understand my situation and forgive me. When I was asked how I knew the details of the incidents to which I had confessed, I told him that Ahmad Trudy, my interrogator, had given them to me.

21. I declare that all the above is true.

22. I declare that this is my name, this is my signature and the content of the affidavit is true.

Signature of Ismail El-Gul

Today, February 9, 1990, I, Attorney Lea Tsemel, met Ismail El-Gul, I.D. 23261480. After I warned him that he must speak the truth and made him aware that he would be punished according to the law if he failed to do so, he swore to the truth of his statements.

Signature of Lea Tsemel

Affidavit 5 June 4, 1991

I, the undersigned, Iad Allami Judah, after being warned that I must speak the truth and knowing that I will be punished according to the law if I neglect to do so, hereby declare:

1. On Sunday June 2, 1991, at 16:00, I was brought into Room 2 of the Russian Compound in Jerusalem. This was only after the policeman brought me to the Registration desk and told another policeman – with a paper – to take me to Room 2.

2. Eight people were in Room 2 when I was brought in and yesterday another person was added – all of them were Arabs. The room was not in the Shabak wing but rather in the prison itself. On the first day the people in the cell did not do anything to me, they only joked around.

3. Yesterday afternoon, after supper, one of the men in the cell, who was tall, a little fat and had a beard, introduced himself as Joseph from Beit Lehem (although his accent was from Hebron) and insisted that I must belong to an organization. I told him that I had never been recruited to any organization. He went to talk to someone else who had introduced himself as Haled Abdallah. Mr Abdallah had black hair, was skinny and approximately 30 years old. He claimed that he was the security person in the room. He also interrogated me and told me that I must tell them which organization I belonged to. I refused. He told me that I had to write a letter claiming that I did not belong to an organization and that I did not belong to the Popular Front. He started dictating what I was to write. I refused to write anything. He asked me why. Later he buzzed and a person named Riad was taken out of the room. After more than an hour, when Riad returned, he said that he had talked to the others; he said, 'it will be okay' and he sat by Joseph. Later, he sat me down in the corner and told me that I must tell him everything. He began to interrogate me and asked me if I knew certain people. These were the same people that the Shabak had mentioned and asked me if I knew during their interrogation of me. He told me that these people were interrogated in the Russian Compound and that they had implicated me. I told my interrogators that they could talk to my lawyer and they told me that they had sent a messenger to notify my lawyer, Lea Tsemel, that I had been transferred to another jail.

4. Later they told me that I had implicated the people whose names were mentioned. And later they said that I was a collaborator.

5. Riad began beating me on my face, he slapped me several times from right to left. He boxed me on my shoulders and in my face and on my head. He hit me very hard on my head with a flat hand and boxed me in the chest while all the others shouted, 'this is a collaborator, we want to kill him and we must kill him'. Riad spat on me three times and threw me to the floor several times. He also kicked me in the chest while I was lying on the floor and he smashed my head into the wall a few times. Later he forced me into the shower.

Following these actions, Riad and two others took me to the shower, took off my shirt and forced me to shower. After that, they told me to get dressed and then hit me again in the same manner as before and they continued to shout, 'Confess, confess, talk about your contacts with them, you are responsible for them and if you won't confess, you are probably a collaborator.'

6. Riad then questioned me about people who had been killed in Ramallah, he asked me whether I had known them or not. I told them that I hadn't known them. The people in the room accused me, saying, 'You don't want to answer, you probably did it.'

In the meantime, all the others were standing around me, cursing me, threatening me and hitting me. Two of them were praying. The one with the beard suggested that I be taken to the second floor and thrown down. After half an hour I was again taken to the shower; at this point I was faint and my whole body hurt. Every time after they took me to the shower to rouse me, they interrogated me again.

7. They conducted a real interrogation. Joseph would start by hitting me on the head very hard until I fell to the floor and then he held the palm of my hand and squeezed my wrist using his fingernails, all the time telling me to confess about my contacts with these people. I want to note that after one of the showers Joseph ripped out some of my moustache hair.

After I returned from the third shower, they were quiet and they talked to me quietly. I told them that I didn't want to talk with them and at midnight they went to sleep. Riad stayed awake with me and he sat me next to him. 'Answer and confess about your contacts with people,' he said. 'It will be better for you.' He talked to me about my wife and said that she had been caught with a paper and he asked me what was in that paper and who had come to my house. He also asked about my activities when I was attending the university. He wanted to know how I met my wife. He knew that my wife was from Jenin.

8. I am showing my attorney the marks of the beating on my head, on my temple, the marks of the beating on my shoulders, the marks of the fingernails on my wrists and red marks on my head and behind my right ear.

9. This affidavit has been given so that it can be presented to any institution and any person.

10. I declare that this is my name, this is my signature and the content of the affidavit is true.

Signature of Iad Allami Judah

Today, June 4, 1991, I, Attorney Lea Tsemel, in the Russian Compound, met Iad Allami Judah who had been identified by the warden. After I warned him that he must speak the truth and made him aware that he would be punished according to the law if he failed to do so, he swore to the truth of his statements.

Signature of Lea Tsemel

Affidavit 6 December 6, 1987

I, the undersigned, Ralid Aziz Jarar, after having been warned by Advocate Felicia Langer that I must testify truthfully or be liable to punishment as stated by the law, hereby testify the following:

1. I, the plaintiff, in the appeal submitted to the Supreme Court of Justice, request that it investigate my complaint concerning the torture I suffered at the hands of the GSS personnel in Jenin Prison. The purpose of this appeal is to

bring the torturers to trial, and this affidavit is written to back and to testify to the truth of the below.

2. I was detained on October 21, 1987 when I was summoned to the GSS offices in Jenin, after which I asked to receive a travel permit.

3. Later I was brought to Jenin Prison where they began to interrogate me on the claim that I am a member of the Fatah organization, a fact which I denied as follows:

a. The interrogators would lay me down on a table with my hands tied behind my back. They placed bags on my head, and would close my mouth and nose until I felt like I was suffocating.

b. The interrogators, 4 or 5, would hold my hands and legs and beat me, also in my groin. These were GSS interrogators.

c. The person that was responsible was named Sammi, another one of them was called Benni, and yet another was called Mike. The fourth person I do not know.

d. The torture described above was repeated three times for a few minutes each time. In the course of the second time I lost consciousness, and the third time was the longest and hardest of them all.

e. I had the feeling that I was dying. The investigators knew that I spoke German and told me, 'Wir sind Hitler Gruppe wirst du die warheit sagen du Schwanz.' Namely, we are the group of Hitler ...

f. For approximately 15 days I was kept in a structure the shape of a closet – 1 meter long and 70 centimeters wide – with a hood on my head. I could hardly breathe in this structure. Although I complained, I did not receive medical attention, although I complained of breathing problems, and pains in my groin area following the beatings I received. I also had head-aches; the doctor gave me an aspirin without examining me.

g. Until this day, I experience back-aches as a consequence of the interrogation.

h. I was very afraid of death, particularly after my interrogators threatened me that 'We killed a person before you.' They threatened me so much, that they would deport me from the area if I would not confess. Today, December 6, 1987, I am talking with my lawyer for the first time

i. I confessed to the GSS interrogators. In order to survive the torture, which I could not endure, I made a false confession.

Everything stated in this testimony is true and correct.

Signature of the testifier Ralid Aziz Jarar

VI Medical form of 'Fitness for Torture' used by the department of interrogation

Dept. of Interrogation
Form of Medical Fitness

No. of prisoner _____ name _____ date _____

1. On _____ I examined the above prisoner and his medical findings are:
   a. _____
   b. _____
   c. _____
   d. _____
   e. _____

2. As a result of the above, the medical limitations on the conditions of imprisonment are:

   a. Are there any limitations to the prisoner's stay in an isolated cell? Yes/No
   b. Are there any limitations to the prisoner's chaining? Yes/No
   c. Are there any limitations to wearing head/eyes cover? Yes/No
   d. Are there any limitations to prolonged standing? Yes/No
   e. Does the prisoner have any physical injuries (before entering interrogation)? Yes/No
   f. Main medical limitation:

   1) _____
   2) _____
   3) _____
   4) _____

Doctor's signature _____

Index